DRAYTON MANOR

George and Vera Bryan's

Memories of a Family Fun Park

Credits

Author **Fred Bromwich** MCIPR

Editor **Helen O'Neill** BA (Hons)

Research **George Bryan** OBE

Research **Vera Bryan**

Research **Colin Bryan** MHCIMA

Dedicated to the memory of

William Edward Bryan and Alfred Cartlidge

Contents

First published in 2006 by
Drayton Manor Theme Park
Tamworth
Staffordshire
B78 3TW

www.draytonmanor.co.uk

ISBN 0-9552779-0-6 978-0-9552779-0-0

Designed and produced by Jennings Campbell Bibby.

Foreword

THE Bryan family's development of award-winning Drayton Manor Theme Park is one of the success stories of the Heart of England and I am delighted to be able to write the foreword for this special publication.

Not only is it a remarkable journey down memory lane, reliving the experiences of its founders, George and Vera Bryan, over the last 56 years, but it also provides a pointer to the future.

The book reflects the genuine enjoyment of millions of families whose visits have helped transform Drayton Manor into one of Britain's Top Five inland tourist attractions – a high quality attraction which, I might add, is the current holder of a "Gold" Excellence Award issued by Heart of England Tourism for achievements in the leisure industry.

Sir William Lawrence, Bt., OBE
Chairman
Heart of England Tourism

DRAYTON MANOR PARK
LAKESIDE RESORT
GREETINGS
FROM
DRAYTON MANOR PARK
INLAND PLEASURE RESORT
FAZELEY NR. TAMWORTH STAFFS.
Skating Rink & Clock Tower
Paddling Pool
Speedy Photo Service
Boating Pool
DRAYTON MANOR PARK
LAKESIDE PLEASURE RESORT
NEAR TAMWORTH
120 ACRES FOR YOUR PLEASURE & ENTERTAINMENT!
PARTY ORGANISERS WRITE OR PHONE TAMWORTH 631.
DRAYTON MANOR PAR
NEAR TAMWORTH
INLAND PLEASURE RESORT

DRAYTON MANOR PARK
PLEASURE GROUNDS

Introduction

Today, more than one million pleasure-seekers a year pass through the gates of Drayton Manor Theme Park in Staffordshire – many of them overseas visitors. But when the park was originally opened to the public in 1950 by its current owners, the Bryan family, the word "tourist" wasn't even in most people's vocabulary!

It was then the unsophisticated era of the day-tripper – when families were happy to take a bus journey into the countryside for afternoon tea and spend a relaxing few hours away from the hustle and bustle of factory life. Not for them the heady heights of Shockwave, which Drayton Manor introduced in 1994 as Europe's only stand-up roller coaster or white-knuckle rides such as Pandemonium, where the world literally turns upside down. Indeed, the thrills and excitement of today's generation of inland theme parks were then still only the stuff of dreams.

So how did it all begin? How did Drayton Manor develop into one of Britain's Top Five inland tourist attractions, winning major leisure industry awards along the way? And what of its future?

It is a fascinating story – one that has been engineered by the ingenuity and enterprise of George Bryan OBE, who co-founded the highly successful business with his wife, Vera, and who, in the following pages, charts the history of one of the Midlands' best-loved leisure venues.

California in England
Dear Friend
We are once again taking this opportunity of extending to all our patrons and friends, past, present and future, our very best wishes for the coming year and hope that we may have the pleasure of your company this year at California.
Many say that our resort is the ideal spot for a children's outing or a pleasant day in the lovely Berkshire countryside.
It is our pleasure to supply, at moderate charges, food and refreshment in clean, modern surroundings for numbers, large and small, and venture to suggest that we have, for the adults, a restaurant and ballroom ideally suited for luncheons, afternoon teas, supper dances or social evenings.
We aim to add fresh attractions each year, to improve upon our services of the past, and to maintain the personal associations which have made us so many friends during the 21 years that California has been open to the public.
CALIFORNIA IN ENGLAND
SAND PIT . PADDLING POOL
SWINGS . MERRY-GO-ROUNDS
SLIDES
ZOO . BOATING . DANCING
CHILDREN'S AMUSEMENT PARK
MINIATURE RAILWAY
PONY RIDES . NOVELTY SHOP
AQUARIUM . PUTTING GREEN
SWIMMING . SNAKE TRAIN
CHILDREN'S BOATING
RESTAURANT AND SNACK BAR
are available at moderate charges
CALIFORNIA-IN-ENGLAND
LTD.
NINE MILE RIDE
Near WOKINGHAM
BERKSHIRE
PHONE: EVERSLEY 2256
CALIFORNIA-IN-ENGLAND, THE PAVILION
CALIFORNIA-IN-ENGLAND, BALLROOM
CALIFORNIA-IN-ENGLAND
IT'S A TREAT FOR EVERYONE
CALIFORNIA
here we come!
CIRCUS under the 'Big TOP'
Showing Dates: 30th MAY–11th JUNE
1st AUG–27th AUG.
(inclusive)
Your enquiry and subsequent entertainment will be the personal charge of Mr. and Mrs. Norman E. Cartlidge
PROPRIETORS
The admission charge of 4d. each for parties of 20 or more covers the following with no extra charge:—
★ Punch and Judy Shows
★ Clown entertainment
★ Swings and merry-go-round
★ Aquarium
★ Paddling Pool and Sandpit
★ Garden and Walks
★ Use of Sports Field
★ Pets Corner
Swimming, Archery, Boating and other entertainments at moderate charges
Everybody's happy at
ENGLAND NINE MILE RIDE . NR. WOKINGHAM
PHONE: EVERSLEY 2256
California in England
YOU'LL FIND US HERE
SLOUGH
WINDSOR
BRACKNELL
READING
ASCOT
WOKINGHAM
NINE MILE RIDE
A222
TO LONDON
BAGSHOT
CAMBERLEY
BASINGSTOKE
MODEL RAILWAY with RESTAURANT and BALLROOM in the background
BATHING
CALIFORNIA IN ENGLAND is a natural beauty spot and Pleasure Park with much to attract both young and old. The 70 acre estate with picturesque lake is wooded by pines and silver birches, not forgetting the rhododendrons which, when in bloom, are alone worth a visit.
CALIFORNIA IN ENGLAND was first opened to the general public in 1930, and since that day has seen over a million visitors. You and your friends can enjoy boating, swimming, dancing, pleasant hours in the children's Amusement Park, and find friends among the animals of the miniature zoo, especially the children who have their own pets' corner. Other attractions include Children's Paddling Pool, Show Boat, Snake Train, and Model Railway, which have become popular with all ages.
CHILDREN BOATING on safe shallow water
WE WISH YOU HAPPY DAYS AT CALIFORNI
CALIFORNIA-IN-ENGLAND, DIRT TRACK
TELEPHONE:
EVERSLEY 2256
CALIFORNIA IN ENGLAND, Ltd.,
WOKINGHAM, BERKSHIRE.
LAKESIDE PLEASURE RESORT.
PARTIES CATERED FOR.
DIRECTORS N. E. CARTLIDGE J. T. CARTLIDGE
G. H. H. BRYAN V. F. A. BRYAN
California-in-England
WOKINGHAM BERKS
CATERING can be undertaken for any number from 1 to 1,000. LUNCHEONS and TEAS are served daily from Easter onwards, and for booked parties throughout the Year. Menus and further details may be supplied on request.
SPECIAL MENUS ARRANGED.
MODERN SPACIOUS BALLROOM
ALL ENQUIRIES TO:
CALIFORNIA-IN-ENGLAND Ltd.,
NINE MILE RIDE,
Nr. WOKINGHAM, BERKS.
Phone: EVERSLEY 2256
CALIFORNIA-IN-ENGLAND
WOKINGHAM BERKS
THE BEAUTIFUL INLAND LAKESIDE PLEASURE RESORT
Why not make California-in-England the place for your Next Outing?
OPEN DAILY AT 10 A.M. FROM EASTER ONWARDS
No admission charge made for entry to the grounds
FREE CAR PARK
PRICE 2d.

Chapter One

Our roots are in California

WHERE would we be without Walt Disney? His legacy to the world of leisure has seen the development of Disney World and Disneyland theme parks in every continent except Central Africa.

Disneyland first opened in 1955. The rest, as they say, is history.

Disney is a truly remarkable empire and although it is several years now since my wife Vera and I last visited America the enchantment of Disney's magical world still lives on in my mind. So do memories of California – though it is not the American sunshine state I am particularly thinking of.

To be more precise, it's California-in-England. That was the name of a wonderful, 70-acre estate of woodland in Berkshire where we served our leisure industry "apprenticeship," Vera, more so than me, because that is where she spent much of her childhood.

California-in-England was, in fact, owned by Vera's father, Alfred Cartlidge. Born within the sound of Bow Bells, he was, by profession, an engineer, highly innovative just like my father. After the Great War, he manufactured 14-seater motor coaches, which went by the splendid name of Crimson Ramblers, and organised trips to the South Coast – but always at the back of his mind was a plan to try to find somewhere nearer to home to take the people. When Parliament passed an Act in 1929 prohibiting the use of coaches on the roads over a certain width that was it. All of Mr Cartlidge's coaches were too wide! So he sold them to a business in Jersey – and then went off to develop his country amusement park in Berkshire.

It was 1931. There was no electricity on the site, no water (apart from a lake, which was used for fishing, boating and swimming), no gas and no sewage. And to cap it all, the country was in the middle of a depression. But Mr Cartlidge told his family: "If we can

LIKE THIS LITTLE CHAP
YOUR KIDDIES WILL ENJOY A TRIP ON
CRIMSON RAMBLER COACHES
"Little Crimson Rambler"
Children under 12 years—half price

3

1 An early portrait of Norman Edward Cartlidge, Vera Bryan's brother

2 Vera Bryan's father – Alfred Cartlidge in Silent Knight Limousine for hire c.1918/9 after the Great War

3 Crimson Rambler in Alfred Cartlidge's brochure with his son Norman sitting on it

4

32-Seater
Crimson Rambler All-weather Saloon Coach.

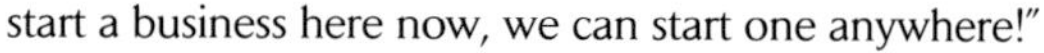

start a business here now, we can start one anywhere!"

How right he was. California-in England was just 35 miles from Hyde Park Corner – and Londoners were soon flocking there for a day out. As facilities improved, he had a paddle steamer and boats on the lake, there was a dirt-track for motorbike meetings, a maple floor ballroom for dancing, tea-rooms and a shop. For 1 shilling (the equivalent today of 5p) visitors could have as much tea as they wanted. But if they wanted scones, cream and jam that was another 3d. And it was 6d extra for egg and chips.

Although there were no mains facilities, Mr Cartlidge was tremendously resourceful. In fact, he dug a well for water and managed to locate a generator which provided the electricity.

Vera, who had left school at the age of 14, was helping with the teas, serving visitors by the lake. As a child, she had been brought up by her grandmother and stepmother, for, sadly, in 1919, when Vera was aged just two years old, her mother died. By the time her grandmother had died in 1935, Vera had taken over the running of the tea shop, with all the responsibilities that that involved.

Then, everything changed again. It was 1939. War was declared – and California-in-England was taken over for a while by the Cameron Highlanders, who marched in on September 3. Vera's brother, Howard, joined the "Terriers" and went off to France. His return after being rescued from the beaches of Dunkirk was made even more poignant when the family heard that

4 Crimson Rambler 32 seater

5 Howard Cartlidge born 1918, killed on manoeuvres in 1940, after serving at Dunkirk, pictured in 1938 at Butlin's Clacton on Sea

6 Young Vera and Cougar 1st in 1944

he had later been killed while on manoeuvres in Devon. A sergeant in the Royal Engineers, he died when the vehicle in which he was travelling overturned. Howard was just 22.

With the outbreak of war, Vera's father went back to being an engineer, shutting down the pleasure park and converting the restaurant into a factory in order to manufacture vital parts for aircraft. Vera herself donned bib-and-brace overalls and spent five years working alongside her father, much of the time as an acetylene welder!

Meanwhile, I, like every other able-bodied teenager at the time, had volunteered to join the Army. It was on my 19th birthday when, in 1940, I found myself in the Royal Warwickshire Regiment. And I can recall doing my "square-bashing" in my own shoes because the Army didn't have a size 12 at the time! But I first saw "action" even before that!

I had joined the Local Defence Volunteers (LDV) at Kegworth (the Leicestershire village where I was

7 George and Vera's wedding photo: Standing row left to right: Herbert Hickman, Ken Potts, Jim Bryan, George, Vera, Alfred Cartlidge, Kate Sheila Bryan, Vicar Henry Lewis who worked at California in England, Norman Cartlidge, Arthur Edward Cartlidge. Sitting row left to right: Squadron Leader William Edward Bryan DFC, Mary Edith Bryan, sitting right of the bride, Edith Rose Cartlidge, far right Olive Edgington

8 Sheila Bryan, Jim Bryan, Mary Edith Bryan, George Bryan, Vera Bryan – Vera's first meeting with her prospective mother-in-law, c June 1942

9 The Cartlidges: Howard, Vera, Alfred, Edith and Norman at the California in England lake, summer 1939

10 George Bryan smiling in uniform after the war on leave in Egypt

11 William Edward Bryan DFC wearing his Royal Flying Corps uniform of the First World War

born in 1921) and when we were on night-time duty some of us spent our time sleeping in an old barn. One night, I will always remember, I was on guard when this huge object in the sky suddenly loomed overhead. I had never seen anything like it before – and quickly woke up the rest of our squad. It was just like a scene from Dad's Army! Were we under attack from some German secret weapon? We didn't know what to think. But we had one shotgun between us – so our marksman fired away. It was only after we had shot down the "enemy" that we discovered we had bagged a barrage balloon that had floated free after an air raid on Derby!

After my short spell of service with the Royal Warwickshire Regiment, I was with the Royal Army Ordnance Corps (R.A.O.C.) and then, finally, I joined the Royal Electrical and Mechanical Engineers (R.E.M.E). And that was wonderful! Like my own father, I had an aptitude for engineering, having been educated at Loughborough College and College of Engineering. But more of my time with R.E.M.E. later on.

These were dark times – but the best thing that ever happened to me took place in May, 1942. I am not a great dancer, but I will always remember a certain dance-evening in the Sgt's Mess at a R.E.M.E. base depot at Arborfield near Wokingham. The base, which even today is of significant importance as a R.E.M.E. HQ location, wasn't far from California-in-England and it was there that I met Vera. We chatted, we danced. I even took two dancing lessons so I could meet her again!

We married the same year – on December 9 – while I was on embarkation leave waiting to go to Egypt. I was just 21. We spent five happy days together in London, visiting the cinema in Leicester Square to see James Cagney in Yankee Doodle Dandy – and opening a large tin of Danish gammon, which Vera's father had saved from somewhere, for our wedding feast!

I spent the next three-and-a-half-years in the Egyptian desert. I was stationed at a R.E.M.E. base depot in Tel el-Kebir – and never once fired a shot in anger! So how did I get to Egypt? Well, after six months at Arborfield, I was fortunate enough to win rapid promotion to the rank of AQMS and was sent off to join a R.E.M.E. attachment to the 27th Lancers based outside Cambridge. I had always been interested in engineering and mechanical matters and it must have been obvious to my superiors. For I was plucked from the classroom at Arborfield – and installed as an instructor, teaching UK and Canadian troops about the maintenance of armoured cars! The first time I set off for North Africa, however, I never actually got there. We had stopped at Lutterworth one night while en route to the coast with the 11th Armoured and it was about three o'clock in the morning when we were awoken to say we were being turned back to base. We found out later that Churchill had cancelled our advance because of heavy rains in North Africa – which almost certainly would have meant that our armoured cars would have been bogged down and rendered useless.

Then, I received a "lone posting" to an unknown destination. All I knew was that I had to report to a ship that would take me and 4,000 other troops to

12 George Bryan on Matchless motorbike in Egyptian desert 1946 with Gerry Sutherland

13 Young Vera Bryan portrait 1943

14 Staff outing from California 1934: Vera's grandmother, Alice Cartlidge far right front row, a year before she died in 1935, Vera's father Alfred Edward Cartlidge in a cap back row fourth from left, Vera's grandfather Arthur Edward Cartlidge with moustache far right back row

goodness knows where. We spent the next two weeks dodging U-Boats before reaching Suez – my gateway to Tel-el-Kebir. This was a huge depot 60 miles north of Cairo in the Nile Delta and it was where, to my great surprise, that I and other senior NCOs were told we would be manning a School of Instruction! By this time, huge numbers of American tanks and armoured cars were arriving to replace the ancient vehicles that our own army possessed.

So it was back to giving quick-fire instructions to "green" troops, who, in just 14 weeks were being turned out as "craftsmen" and deployed to units throughout the Army. That's how the system worked – but it gained me promotion to WO1 – an Armoured Sergeant Major, the highest rank possible for a non-comissioned officer.

It was while at Tel el-Kebir that I witnessed a medical miracle. Many of the troops at the base suffered from very nasty desert sores and had to go over 20 miles away to the 27th General Army Hospital for treatment. Most of them came back cured – laughing their heads off, but with very peculiar tales to tell that most of us found difficult to believe.

Apparently, their treatment involved having a powder sprinkled on their wounds. In no time at all, the sores disappeared. The "magic cure" was penicillin – and it was one of the first times that it had been used.

Come the end of the war, I was still in Egypt. In fact, I wasn't given my demob until 1946 – the year after hostilities had finished. I didn't particularly like that, but that's the way it was for thousands of service-men. I was demobbed with an Army great coat, a suit and a paltry pay-out. Not much after six years of service – and even today I still think it was a disgrace the way that people were treated after finishing their war service. Mind you, the country would have been broke had it not been for the Marshall Plan and lend-lease. I believe that American aid should never be forgotten. But, sadly, I fear it is – apart from being remembered by us "oldies."

Naturally, at the end of the war, I wanted to get back to see Vera – but I also wanted to pick up my life again. Trouble is, I didn't really know what to do. Fortunately, I had both a father and father-in-law whose advice I valued. Both had been forced to start their own lives over again and I knew that whatever they told me, it would be with the voice of experience.

Apprenticed to the great Henry Royce in Derby (a man he described as a wonderful engineer but a hard, ruthless, taskmaster), my father had been a Royal Flying Corps airship pilot in the 1914-18 war, and in the years prior to the Second World War had become one of the country's biggest manufacturers of automatic machines. Thousands of his penny slot machines were in amusement arcades throughout the land – and today they are collector's items.

When war broke out, however, he closed his factory and returned to the RAF, eventually being demobbed with the rank of Squadron Leader.

My father-in-law had worked in the RAE at Farnborough before and during the Great War. Then, after his coach business, he started his pleasure park Sadly he had to close it down in 1939 and then convert some of his buildings into factory space in order to carry out war work.

With hindsight, I don't suppose it was any great surprise that everyone at the "family summit" agreed that my best course of action was initially to return to California-in- England to help both my wife, and her father, re-establish the pleasure park business. After all, when our Dads met up, they got on like a house on fire. With the war-time death of Vera's brother, Howard, tragedy entered our lives in much the same

15

'Phone: EVERSLEY 2256.

CALIFORNIA IN ENGLAND

THE LAKESIDE PLEASURE RESORT

WOKINGHAM BERKSHIRE

Registered Office: EFFINGHAM HOUSE, ARUNDEL STREET, W.C.2.

DIRECTORS: H. E. CARTLIDGE. V. F. A. BRYAN. G. H. H. BRYAN. H. J. CARTLIDGE.

All Communications to: CALIFORNIA-IN-ENGLAND, Ltd. NINE MILE RIDE Near WOKINGHAM, Berks.

Dear Sir or Madam,

Should you not already have heard of CALIFORNIA IN ENGLAND we would like to introduce you to this lovely Pleasure Resort.

California may prove to be the place for which you have long been seeking for your next outing, enabling you to enjoy to the full the beauty of a natural lake and surrounding woodlands, Pine Trees and Rhododendrons. Excellent catering in our spacious restaurant where you can partake of our special teas with Home Made Cakes, Scones and Jam while passing many a pleasant hour among the numerous and varied attractions found situated in parts of the grounds.

Should you be desirous of visiting California we would like to mention that due to the present shortage of Coach transport we would suggest that you made contact with your local coach firm with the least possible delay thus avoiding unnecessary disappointment.

Write for further particulars and menus.

Yours faithfully,

CALIFORNIA IN ENGLAND, LTD.

16

way that most families were affected during those six terrible years, and, sadly, Vera's own mother died when Vera was aged just two, but I have to say that over the years our two families have generated immense happiness. Vera and I have enjoyed 63 years of wedded bliss. It might not be a world record – but it's an achievement of which we are very proud.

Anyway, so California-in-England it was.

We spent our first month together on holiday and went to Devon and Cornwall, having "pooled" everyone's petrol coupons! We took my father's Lanchester car and pulled an Eccles caravan. Our trip took us to a farm on the North Devon coast that Vera's father had bought in anticipation of being able to transform it into a holiday camp after the war. It was in a great spot, adjacent to the beach. But he couldn't get planning permission because eventually a power station was built nearby. So ultimately Mr Cartlidge had to sell. This was a period when Britain was down – and nearly out. You couldn't get hardly anything, let alone timber.

With our holiday over, we returned to California-in-England. Home would be a wooden holiday bungalow, adjacent to the park, which was then owned by our dear friends, Bertie and Flossie Sims, of Teddington. Then we moved to a flat above the shops that had been constructed at the park in 1936. It was there that our son Colin was born. It was a fantastic feeling – after four years of marriage we were a family and planning to open up California.

Life, however, was primitive compared to the sophistication of today. In fact, I think it was "primitive" for about 14 years! For instance, there was no mains electricity or water – just a generator. But things started to improve – and we had two German P-O-Ws who helped me dig trenches so that I could get mains water and power laid on at California.

Pre-war, the generator was always switched off at 6 pm, unless of course, there was a dance either on a Friday or Sunday evening. But once the generator shut down, then oil lamps, candles and primus stoves came into their own.

My wife's younger brother Norman and his wife, Joy, were also running the business with us – and the "rent" we paid to my in-laws supplemented their trips away, most of which were spent in America. Somehow or other, the four of us – Norman, Joy, Vera and myself - managed to source a number of boats for the lake, then we opened up a paddling pool and there was swimming in the lake as well

It was really beginning to take off as a visitor attraction. We had created a ballroom and a restaurant

15 Early mail shot

16 Vera Bryan photographed at 'While u Wait' studio on the promenade in Blackpool.

17 The Pavilion, California-in-England.

18 Model Railway, California-in-England.

19 Tennis hard court, California-in-England.

20 Bathing, California-in-England.

– and I built the park's first "snake train," which weaved its way around the beautiful lakeside setting and was a constant delight to the families who came to California.

Vera had her own key role to play, running the park shop. But she was a devoted mother as well and how she managed to bring up Colin and organise business activities I'll never know!

The two years or so I spent at California-in-England were a real experience. But there is no doubt it provided us with the solid foundation stone from which, later on, we would build our own leisure enterprise. Vera, in fact, spent 17 years at California-in-England and the immense experience she gained in catering and the general running of the park proved invaluable as we set out in business on our own.

Sadly, the California-in-England that we knew as a joyful haven for families in search of a fun-filled day out is no more. The lakeside house built by Vera's father has been demolished. There's no sight of the motorcycle dirt-track, The ballroom, shop and tea-room are just memories.

Today, it is the California Country Park. It's good that it should remain as a green "lung" for recreational pursuits such as walking. But what we helped create has gone. For ever.

21 The Ballroom on the 1st floor of the Pavilion, California-in-England, where George danced with Vera

22 The Showboat, California-in-England.

23 Rustic bridge, California-in-England.

Sir Robert Peel
and Lady Peel
painted by
Joshua Reynolds

24 & 25 Drayton Manor in the 1920s. (Copyright of Tamworth Castle Archives).

Chapter Two

The Peel Estate

I SPENT two years at California-in-England working alongside Vera at my father-in-law's pleasure park and, despite the hardships associated with building a business in post-war Britain, it was an enjoyable – and unforgettable – period in our lives. But as time went on, we realised that what we really wanted to do was to start our own enterprise.

Then, the opportunity came along. I spotted an advertisement in the World's Fair, the leading trade journal for the amusement industry. It said that the derelict Peel Estate in Staffordshire was up for sale. Being a Midlander, I knew of the area and, of course, its connections with one of Britain's most famous families. But the only time I had been there before was as a child when I accompanied my father to a sale of machinery, held on the estate.

The estate was "going for a song." But if it was to "make music" I knew I was in need of some "accompaniment" from my family! It came in the form of funding from my father and father-in-law. Both could see the potential and they put in matching amounts to top up the investment that both Vera and I needed to make our dreams become reality. First, however, something of the history of the estate itself and its special association with Prime Minister Sir Robert Peel, one of the most important men in Britain during the 19th century, and whose memory and achievements live on through the activities of the Tamworth-based Peel Society.

Sir Robert was born in Bury in 1788 into the world of Joshua Reynolds, of stage-coaches and highwaymen, and died in 1850 in the age of Darwin, of Punch, railway excursions, trade unions and income tax. He is remembered for many notable Acts of Parliament and policies, such as the founding of the Metropolitan Police in 1829 and, in the same year, Catholic Emancipation. In 1834 he issued the first party political manifesto, known as the "Tamworth Manifesto."

In his great administration of 1841-1846 he repealed the Corn Laws, which enabled the country's growing working class to enjoy cheaper food, and which, say observers, almost certainly lead to the relative social stability of the UK in the 19th century.

However, Sir Robert is probably best remembered in everyday life for introducing to the streets of London the "Bobby" – a nickname given to the new police in 1829 and one which still exists today.

The Peel family originated in Yorkshire before moving to Lancashire, where they had farming and textile interests and where they did so much to found the great calico-printing trade. The father of Sir Robert later migrated south to Staffordshire and built Fazeley, providing employment for the population of nearby Tamworth. In 1790 he became MP for Tamworth and ten years later was created a baronet.

About this time, he purchased the estate of Drayton Manor, close beside Fazeley, and realised his ambitions to achieve, what The Peel Society describes as, "rank and consequence" in society. Peel passed away at Drayton Manor and, in 1830, was interred in the church at nearby Drayton Bassett – where Sir Robert was buried, in 1850. He died two weeks after falling from his horse in Constitution Hill, London, being so severely injured that he never recovered consciousness.

Sir Robert Peel &
Lady Peel (Beatrice Lillie)
at Drayton Manor.

above
Interior pictures of Robert Peel's house. (Copyright of Tamworth Castle Archives).

Drayton Manor itself was bought by the 1st Baronet in 1790. Later, he demolished the old Tudor property and replaced it with a square Georgian mansion. However, his son, the Prime Minister, did not think it was grand enough and replaced it with his own impressive house, one built by Robert Smirke, the fashionable architect, in the 1830s. The property housed a magnificent collection of rare books and paintings. Sadly, the house is no more. It was demolished in 1926, seven years after the Sir Robert Peel family went bankrupt. But in its heyday it entertained royalty and some of the most important people in the land on more than one occasion. The Duke of Wellington and William Gladstone, who were both in Peel's 1841 government, were visitors. So too was the deposed King Louis-Phillippe of France and his Prime Minister, Francois Guizot, who, in fact, wrote the first-ever biography of Peel. However, perhaps the visit of Queen Victoria and Prince Albert in 1843 was the most memorable. Visitors today can still see tangible evidence of her visit to Drayton Manor; in fact most families follow in the Queen's footsteps when they drive over a bridge – straddling one of the brooks – which was specially built for the occasion; indeed, as was a road leading from the railway station which also crossed our land.

During its history, Drayton Manor also entertained many other notable figures of their day – including the famous Lillie Langtry and Beatrice Lillie who, in 1920 at St Paul's Church, Fazeley, married the fifth Sir Robert – much to the high dudgeon of his father, who really wanted an heiress as his daughter-in-law!

Lillie Langtry, known as The Jersey Lily, was for years the mistress of Edward VII when he was Prince of Wales. Robert Peel, son of the third Baronet, was one of the socialites in the royal circle and he also was one of Lillie's lovers. Apparently, there was once a famous nude picture of Lillie which used to hang – rather discreetly behind a curtain – at Drayton Manor.

Beatrice Lillie was already a favourite with audiences on both sides of the Atlantic when she met – and captivated – the fifth Sir Robert and it wasn't long before they wed. The ceremony, in Fazeley, was attended by a galaxy of stars from the West End stage who later dined on a sumptuous meal in the

Constable J. Bradbury, c.1904

Sir Robert Peel

26 Old Manor House conservatory. (Copyright of Tamworth Castle Archives).

27 Old Manor House drawing room. (Copyright of Tamworth Castle Archives).

28 The former Peel Estate office, one of only 2 surviving buildings along with the Clock Tower, once home to the young Bryan family, and now used as Drayton Manor Theme Park administration offices. (Copyright of Tamworth Castle Archives).

29 Drayton Manor at the time of the visit of Queen Victoria and Prince Albert, 1843.

30 The Drayton Manor site just as it was when George and Vera arrived on October 16th 1949. They made a flat on the upper floor of the former Peel estate office where they lived and raised their family for 10 years! There were no houses around and they needed every penny to get the business going. George's 1st overdraft was for £1500, afforded to him by the National Westminster bank manager Bill Kell.

31 Drayton Manor at the time of Robert Peel's residence.

Statesman's Gallery at Drayton Manor before the happy couple went on spend their honeymoon in Monte Carlo. It wasn't a good idea.

Bobby, as he was known, might have been heir to a baronetcy – but he was heir to precious little else, save his father's love of gambling. So the story goes, he lost so much at the gaming tables that he had to borrow money from his bride in order to pay their hotel bill!

The couple had a son, later to become the sixth baronet, and in 1925 Beatrice – by then one of the greatest singing stars on Broadway – became Lady Peel upon the death of her husband's father. But, even though the Manor was sold, there was still no money and the couple drifted apart, with Sir Robert dying suddenly from appendicitis in 1934.

Such stories will live on – but although Drayton Manor itself is no longer standing, there is one reminder of what was such a superb residence – the Clock Tower and the Estate Office, which today once again incorporates office accommodation, but which is also one of our main kitchen facilities. Sir Robert did leave another legacy, however – some of the magnificent trees that are such an eye-catching feature of the park. Among them are eleven huge Redwood trees, cedars, oaks and horse chestnuts.

It is a legacy that we are continuing. To date, I have planted over 3,000 trees in the grounds of Drayton Manor – silver birch, weeping willows, Lombardy poplars and oaks. All are now of mature size and a delight to behold – though I must admit some served another purpose as well, being planted not for their beauty alone, but also to "screen" the park from the building work that took place after we arrived!

Another continuing link with the past is, of course, The Peel Society's annual dinner at which the guest of honour is usually the Prime Minister of the day. For almost 30 years, the Society has held this prestigious function at Drayton Manor's banqueting facilities.

As an engineer, I must confess I am fascinated by another of Sir Robert's legacies – a magnificent water system which he had used to great effect by harnessing the power of the swiftly-flowing Bourne Brook. The brook was divided at our boundary into three water courses – one fed the Peel factory to drive the looms, another fed Tolson's mill in Fazeley and the third fed directly into the two lakes which today are a magnificent feature of the park. Both lakes were dug out by hand and one is shaped like South Africa. Amazingly, there is a 22ft difference in height between the three watercourses, which all stem from the one brook.

It was a very clever use of natural resources, the results of which we can all see. Out of sight, however, is another of the achievements of yesteryear. Dating back to the Peel era, about 20ft below the ground, is a sewage system and main storage tank that is still in use today – as, indeed, is the water wheel that originally supplied the main house.

31 & 32 Site shots, one of the lake with sunken landing craft, with only the rowlocks showing. It was eventually salvaged and used as a loading platform. George Bryan found 17 army huts on the site; some were stripped down and sold for timber but the nails were taken out, straightened and put to good use.

33 Clock tower and adjacent army huts.

34 The Peel servants at Drayton Manor. (Copyright of Tamworth Castle Archives).

35 – 37 Dramatic demolition shots of Drayton Manor from 1926 – a scrap metal merchant did the job for the lead on the roof.

38 Monkey puzzle avenue, using their popular name, or Aurecaria trees or Chilean Pines, planted by Peel.

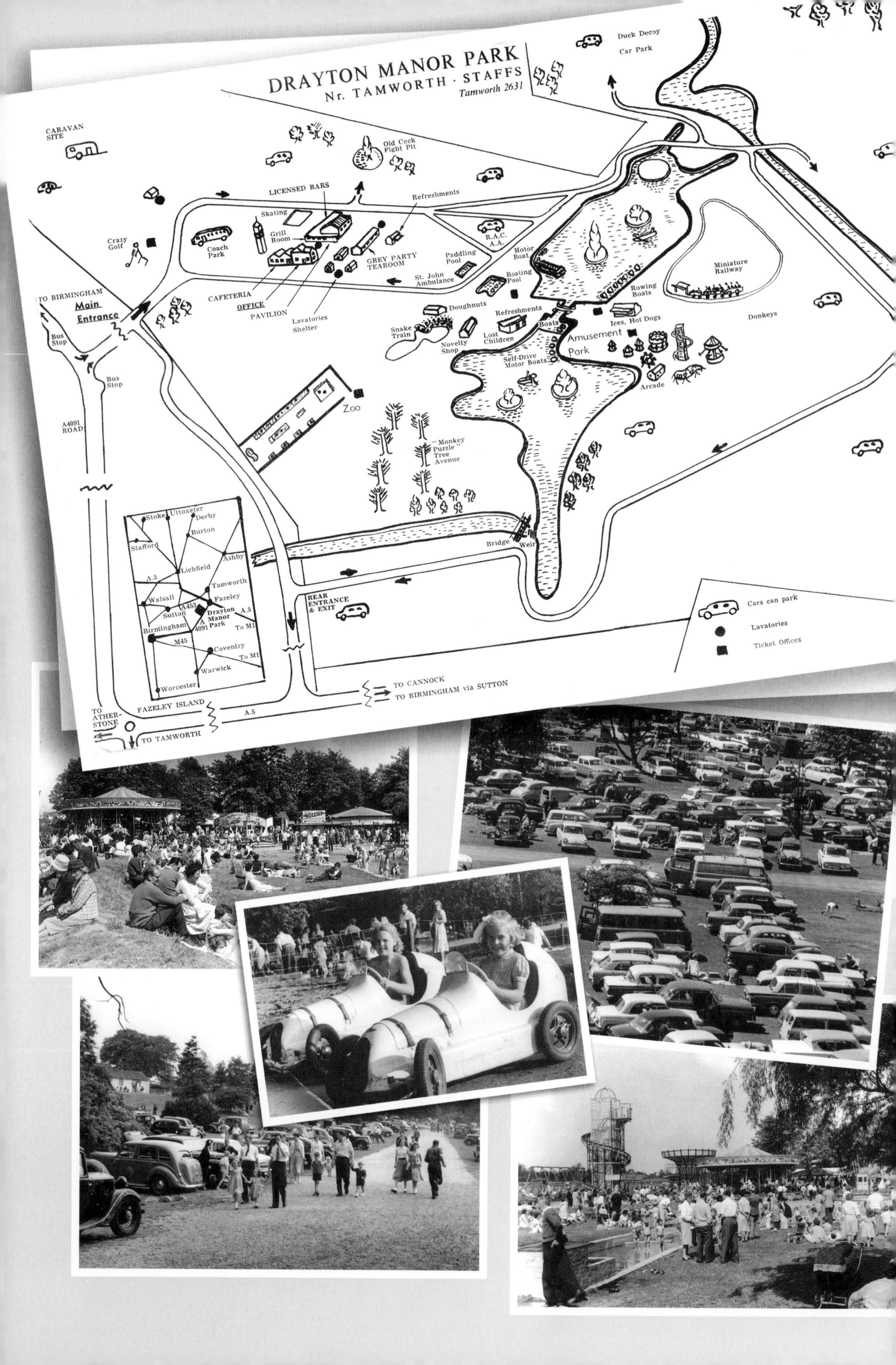

DRAYTON MANOR PARK
Nr. TAMWORTH · STAFFS
Tamworth 2631
Duck Decoy
Car Park
CARAVAN SITE
Old Cock Fight Pit
LICENSED BARS
Refreshments
Skating
Grill Room
Crazy Golf
Coach Park
R.A.C. A.A.
Paddling Pool
GREY PARTY TEAROOM
St. John Ambulance
Motor Boat
Boating Pool
Miniature Railway
Rowing Boats
TO BIRMINGHAM
Main Entrance
CAFETERIA
OFFICE
PAVILION
Lavatories
Shelter
Doughnuts
Refreshments
Snake Train
Novelty Shop
Lost Children
Boats
Ices, Hot Dogs
Donkeys
Amusement Park
Self-Drive Motor Boats
Arcade
Bus Stop
Bus Stop
Zoo
A4091 ROAD
" Monkey Puzzle " Tree Avenue
Stoke
Uttoxeter
Derby
Burton
Stafford
Ashby
Lichfield
A.5
Tamworth
Walsall
Fazeley
A453
Sutton
Drayton Manor Park
A.5
A 4091
To M1
Birmingham
M45
Coventry
To M1
Warwick
Worcester
Bridge
Weir
REAR ENTRANCE & EXIT
Cars can park
Lavatories
Ticket Offices
TO CANNOCK
TO BIRMINGHAM via SUTTON
TO ATHERSTONE
FAZELEY ISLAND
A.5
TO TAMWORTH

39 – 40 Photos taken in Spring 1949, showing the wild, overgrown site and the immense amount of work to be done. An employee called Henry Miles had to cut through the brambles with a motorised Allen Scythe.

41 W E Bryan's Lanchester car parked in the overgrown site.

42 Henry Miles and the Allen Scythe.

Chapter Three

Where it all began

THERE are two dates I shall never forget. October 16, 1949 and Easter, 1950. The first was when Vera and I arrived at Drayton Manor after acquiring 80 acres of land. We had with us our one-year-old son, Colin, who is now the theme park's managing director. The second date was when Drayton Manor inland pleasure resort officially opened to the public.

However, if you had asked me on that first day, when I stood looking at 4ft high brambles, mounds of rubbish, old army huts and pastureland so overgrown it just wasn't true, if in six months time we would be ready to open as a leisure attraction, my first reaction would have been: "No way. It's impossible." The estate was a total rubbish heap when we took it over! Much of the ground was swamped and both lakes were blocked up with all kinds of rubbish. The Army had moved onto the site in 1939 and continued to occupy it during the war, but, after the end of hostilities, it was surplus to requirements.

Initially, people living in the locality thought we were barmy to want to undertake such a project. We were living in a flat above the old Estate Office and only three businesses in the area were prepared to give me credit, ironmonger the late George Felton, nuts-and-bolts merchant Roger Atkinson, with whom I am still friends today, and the late Bill Perkins, whose business as a builder's merchant carries on today in the name of Jewson. But we had a goal. And we proved that nothing is impossible if you really want to succeed.

We lived in that flat for ten years – and living "above the shop" inevitably meant that we worked through the night as well. It has happy memories, however, and our two other children, Jane and Andrew, were both born there.

To say it took a lot of back-breaking hard work to get everything shipshape would be a massive understatement. But with more than a little help over the next few months from my father, his own gang of workers, and local men who eventually joined our team, we got there in the end. A Polish refugee, who had been working for me at California-in-England, also joined the team.

We had to clear the lakes and watercourses of silt and sludge, we had to put down roadways and restore acres of grassland. And we didn't have anything like a JCB digger to help us clear the way. Instead, I remember buying an old Fordson tractor for £5 and

fixing an iron plate on the front, rather like a snow plough. Also, I remember that, thankfully, the Allen motorised scythe had just been invented. It was one of the first machines capable of tackling the "jungle" of grass and brambles with which we were faced. One employee, Henry Miles, whose loyalty I will always remember, spent months cutting away the debris. After scything, Henry would then operate the "Landing Craft" motorboat, which I had made. Henry, who lived on site in a caravan, was an excellent man – who even "sat in" looking after our children.

I also had to get rid of 17 very old, very large, army huts! Sixteen of them were dismantled – -I made long tables out of some of the wood and traded the rest for other supplies. I even sold many of the fallen trees on the estate. Some went to Henry Gould, a local timber merchant who used them for planking, while others went to manufacturers who used them in the production of chicken huts. I even straightened out bent nails so they could be recycled. And I bought three old frying pans for 7s. 6d – one of them could fry 28 eggs at a time! You must remember that in those days, in the wake of the Second World War, Britain was still a destitute country.

It was almost impossible to buy anything new – and food rationing was still in existence. We were truly living in the Land of Make-Do-and-Mend. We had to buy whatever we could – I know I went to Blackpool to buy a second-hand doughnut making machine and I used to scour War Department surplus sales in order to acquire the catering equipment that we needed. In fact, I was a proper "Steptoe" – although I bought a

above Early photo of toddler, Colin Edward Jarrom Bryan, now Managing Director, who helped the workmen clearing the park with his miniature wheelbarrow, much to the delight of his parents.

43 A Fordson tractor which cost £5 was used to clear the site, with a plate attached to the front to make it like bulldozer.

44 The restoration of the clock tower – the oak supports had rotted and the cupola was tilting – the actual clock was made by Smith's of Derby in 1843 and is to be seen in Drayton Manor's Peel museum.

45 Early advertising hoarding for Drayton Manor at a railway station.

46 The first coaches c. 1950 and the clock tower. To the left is the Braithwaite water tank which was left by the army and later removed by blowing it up!

47 Lakeside shot of crowds in 1960s.

1929 Chevrolet lorry instead of a pony-and-cart to transport the ovens, hot plates, crockery and cutlery (all with Army identification numbers stamped on them) that I managed to snap up.

All the equipment I bought, however, was best quality stainless steel. Some of it is still in use today in our ultra-modern kitchens.

And if you are wondering what happened to the remaining army hut, well, it's still in use! The hut was our first-ever tearoom and we have incorporated it into the tearoom complex which serves visitors today.

When we opened, well over half a century ago, visitors were less sophisticated, and less demanding, than they are today – which was all rather fortunate! For our facilities consisted of one tiny restaurant, one tea room, three hand-operated rides, half a dozen rowing boats, some pedal cars and a set of second-hand dodgem cars that I bought in Middlesbrough for £500 after seeing an advertisement in World's Fair, the "bible" of the leisure industry. At the time, the dodgems were the only things I could buy. Hardly surprising, but I have a soft spot for dodgems even now. We hadn't even started to imagine the exciting, spectacular rides of today. But, for the most part, families were just happy and contented to bring along a picnic and relax in the grounds, although I must admit some did bring along their own ropes in order to organise tug-of-war competitions! More sweat and tears that, instead of a relaxing day in the sunshine! Drayton Manor was then more like a park with a small funfair; light years away from the attractions of today.

Our first admission charge was 6d for adults – half price for children. But parties were allowed in for free if they bought a meal in the tea-room. Meals were then priced up to 1s. It was 6d a go on the rides – again, 3d for youngsters. Then, and now, I like to think that our charges have been commensurate with the public's purse.

In those days, Tamworth and Staffordshire still had something like five working collieries and there were dozens of more factories in north Birmingham than there are now. So you can understand why many of the men who worked in such hard-working environments just wanted to get out "in the fresh air" at the

48 1950 Gondolas made by George Bryan.

49 Lake with boys and man fishing c.1966. Two landing craft were joined together to make the early Drayton Queen.

50 George and Vera doing their early accounts.

51 Avenue of the monkey puzzle trees from the Peel Estate, now with children playing.

52 Early shot of the Gallopers, the fire engine ride from Tamworth, the hoop-la run by Mrs.Chaplin and the wheel run by Jim Ray. Geoff Ingram in the light jacket in the centre.

week-ends. Admittedly, Birmingham had its "playgrounds" such as The Lickey Hills and Sutton Park. But Sutton Park only ever served teas in a marquee and I knew we could provide families with more than that! (I will always remember the first organised coach party to visit Drayton Manor. It was a group from Aston Working Men's Club in Birmingham. Some years ago, I recalled details of the visit when well-known Midlands' historian Carl Chinn interviewed me on a BBC Radio WM programme. I said if anyone was listening, who might have been on that particular trip, then they could phone the studio and I would give each of them a family ticket to visit the park. Five people had responded by the end of the programme!)

One of the best men I ever had working for me was ex-miner Geoff Ingram, who became our foreman. Geoff was working as an electrician at one of the local pits when I first met him. He was earning 2s. 6d (12.5p) an hour but what he really wanted was a life away from the mines. I offered him the same money – and he jumped at the chance to come and work in the open-air. Geoff was one of a number of ex-miners who we eventually took on. He was superb at DIY. He had a gift for being able to make, or do, just about anything, and I found his support invaluable. He was the type of man who, if he had been marooned upon a desert island, would have made himself a house out of flotsam! Eventually, Geoff left us to help Molly Banham start up Twycross Zoo – which is itself now a leading visitor attraction.

Geoff lived locally – and today we still have a policy of recruiting our staff from the local community. Indeed, we will always be indebted to the thousands of people from the Tamworth vicinity who have worked with us over the years. Loyalty is one of their many qualities – and I have given up trying to remember how many long service awards we have distributed! Today, we have a workforce of 350-plus and are very proud of our "family," which includes many students who take on summer work in order to

53

54

55

53-54 Whit Monday 1956.

55 Water flowing from the top lake to the bottom lake with the first tea shop, late 1950s; there is no proper paddling pool yet.

56 Geoff Ingram on the William Bell steam train.

57 American-style train with petrol electric engine purchased from Hunstanton pier, driven by Maurice Steward.

58 The Texas Ranger train built in Bristol with a Lanchester engine, driven by Maurice Steward.

59 Sid North and his 7¼″ gauge train which he made himself.

60 Des Lee, Tom's son, driving the snake train.

61 Tom Lee driving the snake train; he worked for George Bryan for over 25 years.

62 Rio Grande, the first Severn Lamb train with the 2 seater carriages which are still called Drayton coaches to this day, driven by Michael Liquorice.

above
Peter Severn-Lamb

63 Snake train pictured where now stands the Lakeside teashop and avenue to the zoo, driven by Jack Brown.

64 Cyril Cox was a snake train driver and foreman for 16 years who started to work at Drayton Manor in c1959. Andrew Bryan is sitting in the right front seat.

65 Harry Price "the plasterer" helped out on the snake train at weekends and loved it. He was based at Drayton Manor during the war with the Royal Army Service Corps.

help them through college. In fact, education is something we value and I like to think that as employers we have been in the vanguard of releasing staff to attend college in order to obtain further qualifications. Indeed, I, my son Colin, grandson William and granddaughter Helen have all attended what is now Birmingham College of Food & Tourism. Grandson Edward went to a college in Bath. I attended the college once a week for two years, later joining the Hotel & Catering Institute and subsequently becoming a Fellow. Helen received an honours degree. And they have also undertaken work experience at Disney and other pleasure parks. So we really do practice what we preach!

Geoff Ingram helped me build some of our early funfair rides, including the very popular "snake-train," and he was there when we bought our first big ride – the Chairlift. The "snake-train" earned its name because of the way it weaved its way around the grounds. I made the carriages from ex-landing craft and other Army surplus. The axles came from bomb-carrying equipment.

Later, I met up with Peter Severn-Lamb, a wizard engineer, whose Stratford upon Avon-based company went on to establish a world wide reputation for its quality products, many of which are now collector's items. His small gauge locomotives and models are in theme parts all over the world. Together, we designed Drayton Manor's popular "Rio Grande" train. Sadly, however, Peter's business went into voluntary liquidation in 2004 – an example of yet another excellent business falling victim to cash flow difficulties. However, I was delighted to see, like the Phoenix, it had risen again in 2005, albeit a company of slimmed-down operations.

Sadly, our own "snake-train" finally puffed its last after 20 years of service, during which time rides foreman Cyril Cox was an absolute wizard in maximising its appeal to the public. Having provided thousands of children – and their mums & dads – with tremendous fun and enjoyment, snaking its way around the acres of parkland, the train fell victim to new rules and regulations. It wasn't easy to see it go; after all, the "snake-train" had been with me since the start.

But if there is one thing that is paramount in this business it is customer safety. Health & Safety rules and regulations are stringent and exacting but they are absolutely vital. In fact, this is an area which greatly concerned my son-in-law, Richard Pawley, and he became a member of one of the founder committees which addressed the Health & Safety aspect of UK amusement parks. He later became Chairman of the British Association of Leisure Parks, Piers and Attractions (BALPPA) and was also a member of its amusement device inspection scheme appeals committee.

Obviously, rules and regulations are in place to safeguard the general public but they are also there to ensure that leisure operators continue to maintain the high standards which have made Britain's theme parks amongst the safest in the world.

66 & 67
Whit Monday 1956.

68 Visitors enjoy a game of cricket.

69 Kids on a Wicksteed slide.

70 Henry Miles steering the 1st boat made from landing craft, with a Seagull outboard motor. Another landing craft was also used as a loading platform..

But back to those early days – when Vera and her band of ladies, all recruited from local families, lined up huge urns of tea and when we operated a machine that buttered and sliced a 4lb loaf. That was real hi-tech for then – and a massive boon, as more and more visitors decided to splash out on sandwiches and afternoon teas rather than bring their own picnic. We bought the bread-slicing machine from Wicksteed Park in Kettering and it served us well for many years. (People today talk enthusiastically about such-and-such being the greatest thing since sliced bread. For us, our machine was the best thing BEFORE sliced bread. Well, almost, for sliced bread was first introduced in the UK in 1930.

Incidentally, that well-worn expression, "the best thing since sliced bread," was coined in the US in around 1933 by which time 80 percent of the bread sold in the US was pre-sliced and wrapped! I don't know how much a loaf of bread cost in those days but no-one then could ever have imagined that a loaf of "designer bread" would retail in London supermarkets, as it does today, for almost £10!)

It wasn't long before we could see that Drayton Manor was really becoming a very popular attraction with families living within the Birmingham and Tamworth area. We even made a tiny profit after our first year. Our accountant couldn't believe it! It must have been all those ham salads we sold for 1s6d (7.5p) – a charge that included admission to the park as well! However, I readily admit that there have been some dreadful times as well – many of them associated with our very changeable weather. Talk about the Great British Summer. I tell you, there have been a few that have grated on me!

As time progressed, however, we were up to serving 2,000 teas every Saturday and were becoming increasingly aware – and excited – that Drayton Manor had the potential to develop into a playground for the whole of the Midlands, and even beyond. Strangely enough, at first, we didn't know how to describe ourselves! We weren't a tourist attraction. I don't think tourism was really born in this country until the Duke of Bedford opened Woburn Abbey to the public. In my book, that's when the words "tourist" and "tourism" entered our every-day vocabulary.

Anyway, we decided we would be an "inland pleasure resort." Today, the industry has evolved and we now run a "theme park" – not just for the thousands of thrill-seekers who love the big rides, although they make up a significant proportion of our visitors, but for the family as a whole. Youngsters are especially important to us – and I have always made sure that children aged four and under go free on our rides.

After a while I managed to obtain some children's paddle boats and even some rowing boats – so we dug out a pool, largely by hand shovel. We also introduced a paddling pool and that was quite an attraction in itself. The pool was laid by one of the best plasterer-tilers I have ever come across – Harry Price, who seems to have helped me at the park for ever. The 50s also saw us launch a roller skating rink – I remember buying the roller skates second hand after Dudley Skating Rink closed down – and we purchased motor driven hire boats after opening up a second lake. There was even an 18ft motor boat which we created from an ex-Army landing craft.

We started donkey rides for the children – we even had a donkey cart! And Punch & Judy Shows were also in full swing as the public suddenly found itself demanding more and more.

However, it was in 1954 that we began to expand the operation in quite a significant manner. It was the year we built our first self-service cafeteria – a facility that was still quite rare. In fact, it was such a departure from what most people had been used to, that even cafeteria staff couldn't quite get used to the idea that they no longer had to wait on people! Then, I built the Tower Party Tearoom – and at weekends we were serving 2,500 teas to Sunday School children and parties from Working Men's Clubs.

In 1959, I linked up with Jim Shipley, a member of one of Britain's great fairground families. Jim took a ten-year lease to run the amusements arcade at Drayton Manor, including the amusements I had collected, so taking over a part of the business which I had developed over a period of time. But this was a move that allowed me to concentrate on the expansion of Drayton Manor as a whole. Jim was an extraordinary showman. He even introduced bingo to Drayton Manor – and today the Shipley family is one of Britain's biggest bingo operators.

My father loved the amusements arcade. You'll find out why in a later chapter.

Jim Shipley's arcade brought in even more customers. The whole place was beginning to buzz and on Bank Holidays 6,000 visitors used to flock through the gates. There were families everywhere and everyone wanted to work for us. No longer were we the people who paid "Micky Mouse wages." Today, we have 22 managers and over 350 employees on the payroll.

Then, however, we were still in a post-war era and it wasn't until the end of the 1950s that we were able to significantly increase our facilities by buying 13 new

71 Girls enjoying donkey rides, c.1964/5

72 Paddle boats

73 Punch and Judy was run by a teacher, Mr John Varley. He eventually went to Hong Kong to teach special needs children.

74 George Bryan and Miss Great Britain and her entourage. They opened the Chair Lift Easter 1964, a ride which cost £36,000 to buy and fit. And then of course, the open-top urinals had to have a roof installed so overhead Chair Lift customers couldn't peek in!

75 When Dudley roller skating rink went bankrupt, George Bryan bought all the skates and Harry Price laid the concrete for Drayton Manor's rink. Four roller skating dance champions pictured c.1959/60 Mr and Mrs Ray and Joan Paling (right) National Skating Association bronze medallists, and Richard Twigger, 22 yrs and Janet Blakeway, 19yrs.

rides, one of which was a 19th century-built carousel – and one which is still going strong today. We invested big-time in a new chairlift, which was officially opened by Miss Great Britain. The attraction itself cost £27,000 to buy and install – but there was an additional cost of several hundreds of pounds on top of that which we had not been expecting. We hadn't realised at the time, but those who were airborne when the chairlift was in full swing had a bird's eye view of the gents' urinals – which in those days were open-topped. Hence the unexpected expenditure on a hurriedly erected roof for the toilet block.

An amount such as £27,000 was a huge sum of money then – but we were excited at the future prospects of the park and both of us agreed that financial risks had to be taken.

After visiting Disney World in Florida in 1975, Vera and I further realised that on-going investment was essential if we were to maintain the impetus that was propelling us towards being a major player in the UK leisure industry. We knew, of course, we could never be another Disney – but we could implement some of his ideas! For instance, we wanted to introduce a Jungle Cruise on our smaller lake. The problem was knowing someone who could construct it. One day, a man named Alan Hawes called into the park. He said he could build the Jungle Cruise. And he did – with enormous success. When John Noakes of TV's Blue Peter fame officially opened the attraction, 6,000 people turned up to see him.

We took another step forward in 1960 when we redeveloped the tearoom into a ballroom and added the Tower Lounge. Fully licensed, of course. Ten years later, the Hamilton Suite opened. However, the 70s was not a particularly happy decade and it was one that put us severely to the test. For instance, the OPEC price war saw an end to party group catering, there were strikes, powers cuts and countless other problems and it was not until the early 80s that the economy really started to move again.

We had always been prepared for hard work – and hard work it was. There were times when Vera and I worked around the clock. For instance, when Vera wasn't organising the catering and supervising the staff she was making curtains and other furnishings for the tea-rooms and restaurant. And by now, of course, we also had two more children, Jane, who was born in 1951 and Andrew, who was born in 1954.

There are no short cuts in this, or any other game, if you want to be successful. But we had a vision – and we knew just where we wanted to go. We remained committed throughout, even though at times we wondered whether we would get there.

If there's any advice I can offer to today's would-be entrepreneurs, I would say: remain true to your ideals, don't be put off by hard work – and don't be afraid to seek advice from your seniors.

TELE. TAMWORTH 631.

INLAND PLEASURE RESORT

FOUND ON ANY MAP

Drayton Manor Park Ltd.

NR. TAMWORTH, STAFFS

DIRECTORS: G. H. H. BRYAN, V. F. A. BRYAN

12 ACRES LAKES

70 ACRES WOODED GRASSLAND

Dear Sir or Madam,

We have pleasure in informing you that DRAYTON MANOR PARK is again Open, under new proprietorship, after its long war service.

This 80 acre estate of Beautifully Wooded Grassland has a Large Boating Lake and an Ornamental Fishing Lake. With the Lakes, very rare and impressive Trees, Avenues, etc., it gives one chance of unsurpassed walks.

For the Children, for whom we always make special efforts, there are numerous Free Amusements and a large, very shallow (18″) Children's Boating Pool, a Motorboat, a Snake-train and so on. A Large Field is for the entire use of Party Organisers who wish to run Sports, etc.

The Adults, apart from the Boating, etc., may like to indulge in the very excellent Fishing in the well-stocked Lake. A charge of 2/- per day is made for this popular pastime.

We have no restrictions, there are no traffic or other dangers, we are sure you could give your party the day out they so much desire and with so little worry. There is ample shelter in case of rainy or cold weather.

We can Cater for Large or small Parties, a sample menu being Tea, Bread and Butter, Jam or Paste, and Cakes for Children's Tea at 1/3. Their Lunch 1/8 or 2/-. Adults Plain Tea 1/6, and so on. All Parties of 20 or over (or by special arrangement) booking one meal have FREE Admission to the Grounds. Usual Prices of Admission 3d. and 6d.

We are on the main Tamworth-Birmingham road and Bus routs. You can find us on any map.

You could have a grand time in this beautiful place, in fact, enjoy yourselves in the "Drayton Manor."

Further particulars gladly supplied.

Yours faithfully,

G. H. H. BRYAN
V. F. A. BRYAN.

back Letter from George and Vera Bryan announcing the re-opening of Drayton Manor and a booking form.

76 Family enjoying a picnic.

77 Customers amused themselves with Tug of War in the 1950s.

"...... and thank you for the good service given".

Holy Cross Mission Church Dudley.

"......the praises of your arrangements have been sung by all concerned, so much so that I have had to promise to bring all again next year".

Hill Vicarage,Sutton Coldfield.

"We have this year brought two Sunday School Outings to you and I should like to say how much we have enjoyed them......your meals were excellent value...the many things which children can do without paying are almost unique and they were given a very liberal money's worth on the things for which they pay. Your enterprise is certainly its own advertisement......

St.Thomas' School,B'ham.1.

"......Thank you and your staff for all your help to make our visit enjoyable.

Bedworth Labour Club.

"......on behalf of all the adults I would like to thank you for the splendid meals you provided both for us and the children.... if I can recommend Drayton Manor to anyone you can rest assured I shall do so.

Norman Street, Winson Green.

"......that they all enjoyed themselves and had a very nice tea. Both children and adults were overjoyed with everything".

Salvation Army.Weoley Castle.

"May I express my thanks and appreciation for the excellent day we spent last Wednesday. The kiddies really enjoyed the day and we look forward to visiting you at a later date".

Sunday School,Alvechurch.

"......we consider the prospects very attractive and inviting".

Sunday School,Smethwick.

"......we have been recommended to write to you".

Re National Saving's Rally.

"......as we thoroughly enjoyed our outing and were only sorry we were unable to spend more time in the open."

Parish Magazine.Castle Donington.

"......as Drayton Manor is now occupied by Mr and Mrs Bryan who's ancestors have been so closely associated with our Church. After tea the children proceeded to enjoy the many attractions which are spread around the charming woodland and lakes. All were loathe to return."

St.Clements School.Nechells.

From two scholars. "....thank you very very much for it was lovely...." We did enjoy coming.Thank you for arranging the Sports Ground for us...."
The Headmistress. "I should like to endorse these statements.....thank you most sincerely for the excellence of the catering.Most certainly we look forward to our next visit.

The Vicarage. Cannock.

"......and again saying thank you, in spite of dismal weather everyone enjoyed themselves, the children asking " can we go again next year which is alway's a good sign."

back Endorsements from the 1950 season.

78 Coaches and buses bring the many visitors.

79 Paddle Boat Pool, 1956

80 Sir Robert Peel's Garden Centre was for his own flowers and vegetables; it was bought in the early 70s by George Bryan, and run by Sid Harris.

81 Grey party tea room, now the site of the Cedar fish and chip shop, one of the many structures built by joiner Ron Twomlow.

Drayton Manor Park Limited
Nr. Tamworth, Staffs. **Tel.: TAM 631**
ALL PREVIOUS TARIFFS CANCELLED

Party Catering

Children : *(All children must sit together)*

LUNCHEONS

Fried Fish, Potatoes, Sweet, Fruit Squash ...	2/-
Cold Meat, Tomato Salad, Potatoes, Sweet, Fruit Squash	2/2

TEAS

Tea, Bread and Butter, Jam and Paste, Cakes	1/3
Tea, Bread and Butter, Jam and Paste, Cakes, Jelly	1/7
Tea, Bread and Butter, Jam and Paste, Cakes Ice Cream	1/7

★ ★ ★

Adults :

LUNCHEONS

(A limited number served each day without booking)

Fried Fish, Chipped Potatoes, Sweet, Bread and Butter, Tea	3/-
Cold Meat, Green Salad, Potatoes, Sweet, Tea Soup, **6d.** extra.	3/3

TEAS

Tea, Bread and Butter, Jam, Cakes	1/6
Tea, Bread and Butter, Jam, Assorted Sandwiches, Cakes	2/3
Cold Meat, Salad, Bread and Butter, Cakes, Jam, Tea ... ... Ice Cream, **6d.** extra.	3/6

★ ★ ★

Please use the Booking Form to indicate meals required. Your stated Meal Times will be adhered to as far as possible. Right is reserved to amend these Menus and adjust the price accordingly if food restrictions and/or food prices compel. Additional Menus can be arranged.

★ ★ ★

REFRESHMENTS - CUPS OF TEA - CIGARETTES SWEETS - MINERALS - POSTCARDS - NOVELTIES ICES - ETC. - ARE ALWAYS ON SALE AT THE LAKESIDE SHOP

Prices

Admission :

(Applicable Weekdays, Sundays and Bank Holidays)

Adults	**6d.**
Children	**3d.**

Parties of 20 or over booking meal by pre-arrangement admitted **FREE.**

Cars, Coaches and Cycles
Admission and Parking **FREE.**

Snake Train	Adults **6d.**, Children **3d.**
Motor Boat	Adults **6d.**, Children **3d.**
Adults Rowing Boats ...	2/- 40 mins. (max. **3** in a boat)
Children's Boats (on Shallow Pool) ...	Children **6d.**
Pony Rides	Children **6d.**
Donkey Cart	Children **6d.**
Pedal Car Arena	Children **3d.**
Boat Swings	**6d.** per Car
Swan Boats	Children **3d.**
Putting Green (when completed)	**6d.** per Person
Fishing	**6d.** per Round
Playing Field	2/- per Rod per Day
Swings, Slide, etc.	Free
Swimming	Free
Paddling	Free
Sandpit	Free
... ...	Free

Additional Amusements may be added during the Season.
Right is reserved to amend these prices if conditions compel.

★ ★ ★

THE DANCE HALL which serves also as our second Party Tea Room, is available for Party or Private Hire. For Terms and Conditions please apply.

Chapter Four

More than just tea ...

TONY BLAIR'S Labour Government has been responsible for the introduction of significant new changes to the country's licensing laws – laws which will allow round-the-clock drinking. However, it was the changes to the licensing laws made by Harold McMillan's Tory Government in the 1960s that steered Drayton Manor in a new direction.

When McMillan relaxed the rules it became easier to obtain a licence. So that's what we decided to do – operate licensed premises from within Drayton Manor. We had no desire to run our own pub but we now had the opportunity to provide even yet more facilities for the public.

From teas and tug-of-war on the lawn we went to drinks and dinner-dances in the ballroom!

Dancing has been one of the joys of Vera's life ever since being a youngster, so you can image her pleasure when we decided to launch our own ballroom.

back Prices and menus from the 1950s.

We had, over the years, built up a permanent catering workforce of about 60 full-time people. Now we would have to hit the recruitment trail again as another aspect of business life at Drayton Manor began to take hold. Evening functions, dances and anniversary parties were creating a whole new aspect of our business.

Ever since our first opening day we have embarked upon a programme of continual improvement and development, so when the changes to the licensing laws came into being we were ready. Then, we just had one function suite – after having turned a tea-room into a ballroom in 1960. It was what the public wanted – and we were inundated by companies wishing to stage their annual works dinner dance at Drayton Manor.

And we also attracted the popular big band names of the day. Victor Sylvester (he always liked egg-and-

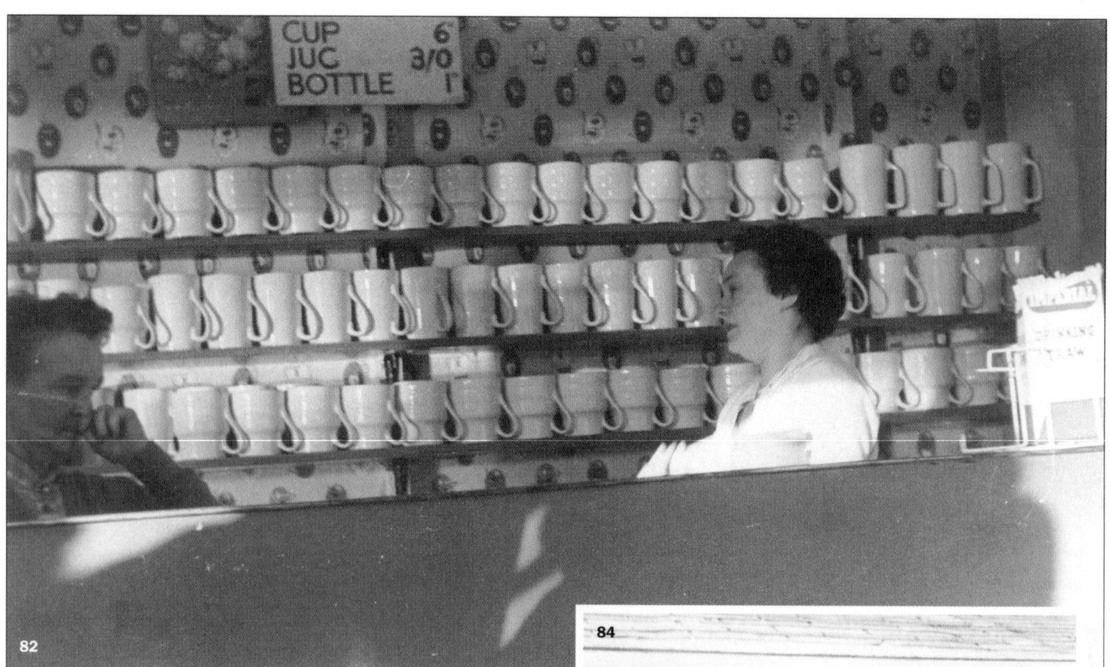

82 Mrs North and Vera Bryan with rows of tea mugs ready to serve the visitors.

83 Tower tea room 1956, now the Tower Ballroom.

84 1951/52: tea ladies in overalls ready to serve.

85 A ladies outing to the grey party tea room. Coach trips were very popular as Drayton Manor was an ideal stop off point between North and South.

86 Victor Sylvester, (standing right) with local band leader Bob Mason (left) Sitting at the piano is the then Managing Director of the Tamworth Herald newspaper Ray Jones, and second from right on the trumpet Brian Bennett.

87 Victor Sylvester and Oscar Deutz on violin.

chips for his meal), Edmundo Ross, Joe Loss, Kenny Ball and Acker Bilk, to name but a few. Entertainers lost on today's generation, maybe, but they were the leading stars of their era.

Today, we have three function suites, the flagship of which is the elegant Tower Suite, and an "army" of part-time staff who are on duty at the numerous evening events that are held every year. Annually, about 200,000 people make use of our facilities, which, in addition to private functions such as anniversary and birthday parties and wedding receptions, cater for corporate dinners, conferences, exhibitions and product launch events. For almost 30 years, The Peel Society has held its annual dinner here, a function at which leading politicians, such as Enoch Powell, Lord Hurd, Harold Wilson and Michael Heseltine, have been the guests of honour. Such events have experienced rapid growth in recent years to the extent that non-leisure park activities now account for 35 percent of our turnover.

Telephone : TAMWORTH 631.

Drayton Manor Park Limited

Inland Pleasure Resort

FFS.

88 Tower tea room with seersucker table cloths made by Vera Bryan.

89 Wedding in Tower Ballroom with cigarettes on the table!

90 Kids enjoying a tea party.

91 Tower tea room: hundreds of Sunday School children enjoy their annual treat, with Mrs Matthews pictured in white.

92 Paintings of Disney characters were found in the army huts, the artistic work of Polish refugees from World War II.

Drayton Manor Park Limited

Nr. Tamworth, Staffs. Phone: 631.

Tariff

Children's Menu:

(All Children sitting together)

LUNCHEONS

Fish Cake, Vegetables, Sweet 1/8

Cold Meat, Salad, Potatoes, Bread and Butter, Sweet 2/-

TEA

Tea, Bread and Butter, Jam, Cakes 1/3
Jelly **4d.** extra.

★ ★ ★

Adult Menu:

LUNCHEONS

Fish and Chips, Sweet, Tea 2/9

Cold Meat, Green Salad, Potatoes, Sweet 3/-
Tea or Coffee extra.

TEA

Tea, Bread and Butter, Jam, Cakes 1/6

Tea, Bread and Butter, assorted Sandwiches, Cakes 2/-

Cold Meat, Salad, Bread and Butter, Scones, Cakes, Tea 3/6

★ ★ ★

★ **Additional Menus can be arranged.**

Prices

Admission:

Adults .... 6d.
Children .... 3d.
Parties of 20 or over booking meals have Free Admission.

Cars, Coaches and Cycles
Admission and Parking Free.

Snake Train .... Adult or Child **6d.**

Motor Boat
Adults .... 6d.
Children .... 3d.

Lake Boats
Adults only (Maximum 3 in boat) **2/-** half-hour

Children's Boats
(Maximum 2 in boat) .... **6d.** per boat

Fishing .... **2/-** per Rod per day.

Sports Field .... Free use.

Swings, Slides, etc. .... Free.

Swimming .... Free.

Paddling .... Free.

Any additional amusements added during Season— at our usual low rates.

Refreshments, Cups of Tea, Ices, Minerals, etc., always on sale at the Lake Shop

Right is reserved to alter any items should

back Pale blue Inland Pleasure Resort leaflet with menus and tariffs.

93 Tea Shop with doughnuts and a little boy marching …notice W E Bryan's Breezy Toys on top of the sign.

94 Tower Suite all laid up with white table cloths c.1971 Vera made the curtains.

95 Exterior of Tower Suite 1961.

96 Tower ballroom c1961.

We can serve up to 950 meals at one function – and there aren't many establishments in the region which can offer that sort of facility, complete with free parking for everyone!

In fact, one of the biggest spectaculars we have ever staged was held on Saturday, August 13, 2005, when the park hosted a VE Day 60th anniversary celebration. The event was a sell-out, attended by 5,000 people, and nostalgia was king as we hosted an unforgettable night with the sounds of Glenn Miller, marching bands, a spectacular firework display and a Spitfire fly-past.

97

98

97 & 98 Tower lounge and bar 1961.

99 Purpose-built self service cafeteria before the Missanda floor was laid.

100 The Missanda Suite, named after the wood used for the floor, serves as the cafeteria in the theme park's summer season, and as a successful ballroom for functions in winter.

101 A Cracker Barrel cheese spread 1970s.

102 Centre is the late Sir David Lightbown, Treasury Minister and then MP for Tamworth, George and Colin Bryan, and Pudsey bear and Drayton Manor's then mascot Rory the Lion. This was to celebrate a £400,000 refurbishment and re-launch of the Tower Suite.

103 & 104 Modern function rooms with decorations.

105 In 1971 purple tower lounge designed by Edward Lyon, of Heals of Tottenham Court Road, London.

106 Tower Suite with theatre style seating, 1996.

107 Entrance shot from 1980s.

108 August Bank Holiday car parks 1988.

VE Day celebrations, 2005

Bryans

"FRUITBOWL"

With or Without Token Prize Payout

This machine is single slot Penny Play 2-12 pa
unusual Player appeal.

Behind the large diameter glass is seen a saucer
colourfully decorated with Fruit symbols and motifs

On inserting coin and turning the handle, the
high speed. The Bowl then suddenly assumes an os
eventually coming to rest. The payout is instanta
matic, depending where the Bowl stops as indica
pointer.

*A Token Payout Unit can be fitted to this mac
extra, this enables a successful player to claim a pr*

The mechanism is basically that of our we
Clock machine, and is fitted to the front panel
case which is readily removable for servicing.

BRYANS 1p CLOCK MACHINE

2-10 PAYOUT

This attractively styled case of polished hardwood is suitable for *wall or counter* fixing, as the cash till *and* the mechanism are accessible from the front.

For servicing, the front panel, together with the mechanism, can be removed without disturbing the case, and placed on the bench.

Height 32″ (81.3 cms.)
Width 18½″ (47 cms.)
Depth 11″ (27.9 cms.)
Weight 60lbs. (27.3 kgs.)

The play is extremely simple. The Player inserts the
turns the key which "winds up" the Clock. The hands
high speed to the accompaniment of a "tick-tock" sound
hands stop. If the Minute Hand stops on any of the twel
the machine automatically pays out the number of coins
the dial—there is no confusing chart to refer to.

The photographs overleaf graphically illustrate
hard-wearing qualities of the mechanism There are *no* coin slides,
the payout system is 100% jam-proof.

BRYANS WORKS
KEGWORTH, DERBY. DE7 2EU. ENGLAN
Telephone: Kegworth 2227 (050-97 2227)

Bryans All-Square Sa

BRYANS ALL-SQUARE SAW

A Combination Tool which is :—

A SAW
RULE
SQUARE
PROTRACTOR

FULLY EFFICIENT FOR EACH USE

Patents and Designs applied for; Copyrights reserved.
The Invention of W. E. BRYAN, the proprietor of :—
BRYANS WORKS,
KEGWORTH, DERBY, ENGLAND.
MANUFACTURERS OF NOVEL MACHINERY.
Established 1920.
Telephone: Kegworth 27.

(BRYANS)

PAYRAMID

A Distinctive and interesting game of skill with Adjustable payout.

The new Payramid combines all the good features of the well-tried and proved model with many modifications and improvements in design, materials and appearance.

In of b are time by t

T deav balls Swin oper knob

The standard machine is constructed to operate
pennies, with instructions in English; but can be
work on other coins, with lettering in any language
ment.

The payout is fully automatic and obtained by
one and only handle. The coin-container and the
self-loading and self-setting, after paying out.

THE PAYOUT IS COMPLETELY ADJUST
moment, without use of tools, and incorporates Br
well known and proved spring controlled coin-hop
out system. The range of payout is from simple
through 2; 1-2; 1-2-3; 2-4-6; 2-4-6-8; or 3-6-9-12
without the Jackpot. The Jackpot can also dis
prizes, such as cigarettes, by separate loading.

Bryans Magic Machines

A series of Coin Operated Machines for the entertainment, education and amusement of all.

Comprising Modern Models, Illustrations, Puzzles, Conjuring Tricks and other Tricks mechanically performed.

BRYANS MAGIC DISAPPEARING DISC.

Patent number 498178, other patents pending.
Registered Designs applied for. All Copyrights reserved.
Invented, designed, manufactured and distributed by
W. E. BRYAN, the sole proprietor of
BRYANS WORKS,
KEGWORTH, DERBY, ENGLAND.
Established 1920. Telephone: Kegworth 27.
Telegrams: "Bryan, Kegworth, Derby."

BRYANS KIDDIE-RIDES

(Bryans) SOLO-RIDE

A Coin-operated Riding Device for the amusement and
tertainment of children aged 2 to 12 years.

his Ride consists of a small model horse, of robust
uction and profiled in shape, with patch legs, beautifully
ted and harnessed, mounted upon a base in which is
d the operating mechanism.

e mechanism is driven by an electric motor and provides,
will of the rider, or person in charge

A SIMPLE WALK AND ROCK.
GALLOP AND TROT.
HUNTING ACTION AND STEEPLECHASE.

ese three entirely different and distinct riding actions
the machine to cater for the nervous, and the bold ; the
, and the twelve-year old. The choice of these actions
ned by moving the lever at the top of the control tower.

Bryans
"SATELLITE"
A Two-Player Table Machine

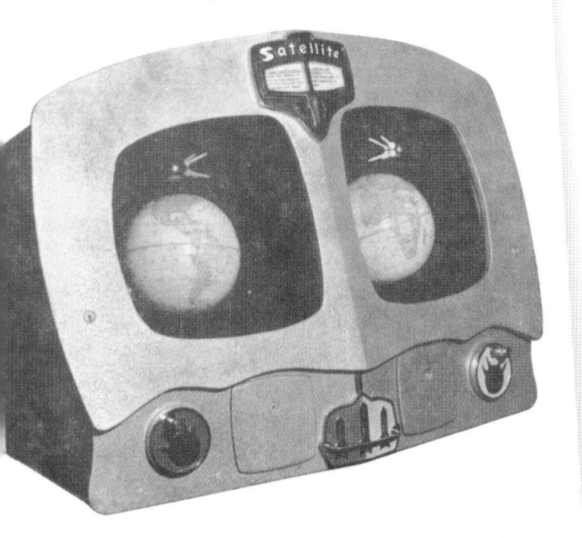

Bryans SATELLITE has been designed to fulfil the need for an entirely new, topical, colourful, bright and excitingly competitive machine for two players, suitable for all locations.

In play, two chrome-plated spherical satellites trailing coloured antennae, encircle two slowly revolving multi-coloured globes representing the Earth.

Surrounding the globes and satellites is a parabolic universe of shimmering, sparkling acetate.

The players insert two coins, then each turns a handle, not too fast, not too slow, but just right, and the player who first succeeds in causing his satellite to encircle its globe receives one coin. There are separate return coin slots for each player, and another slot for a draw or tie.

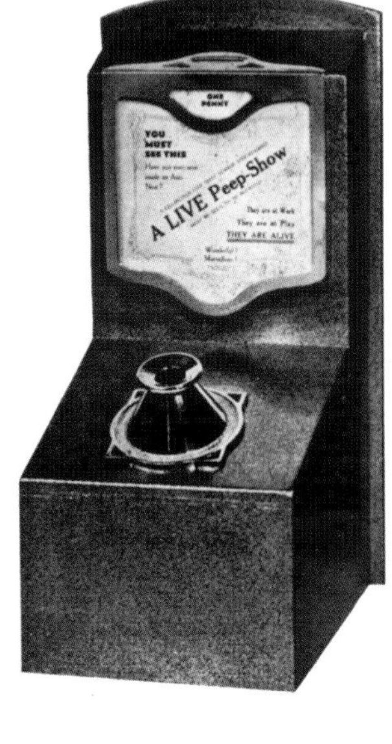

Chapter Five

King of the Penny Arcade

I HAVE referred earlier to the pioneering efforts of Vera's father, Alfred Cartlidge, in establishing the Berkshire pleasure park, California-in-England, and the inspiration and enthusiasm which he generated in ourselves, which convinced us to follow in his foot-steps in the leisure sector.

But my own father, Leicestershire-born William Edward Bryan, was also a leading figure in the amuse-ment industry – and, as visitors to Drayton Manor will discover today, his craftsmanship still lives on. To me, he was the King of the Penny Arcade and many of his original machines are on display in our museum, which opened in 1990, dedicated to the memory of my father and that of a by-gone era.

One of the features of the museum is my father's original workshop - complete with tools, workbench and a coin-operated rocking horse - which we rebuilt to coincide with the official opening of the museum.

William E Bryan was born in 1894 and came from a fairly affluent family; my great-grandfather being Robert Bakewell a renowned agriculturalist and pioneer of scientific stock breeding, about whom it has been said that he did more to revolutionise English farming in the 18th century than any other man. A pioneer of animal genetics, Bakewell lived at Dishley Grange, just north of Loughborough, where, using innovative breeding techniques, he managed to change the shape of animal livestock by creating faster maturing animals with more flesh. He not only challenged formal breeding methods but also the understanding of genetics. And it is said that without Bakewell's livestock there would not have been enough meat to satisfy the population of the Industrial Revolution.

But back to my father. When the First World War broke out, the knowledge he had gained at Rolls Royce, where he was apprenticed to Henry Royce himself, was put to good use and he became a mechanic with the airship branch of the fledgling Royal Navy Air Services. But in 1918 he was transferred as a sub-lieutenant into the newly-formed RAF. It turned out to be quite an eventful year. On one occasion he crash-landed his plane into the end of St Leonard's Pier - but he also established an endurance record (a record which lasted for 12 years) of 50 hours and 55 minutes for the longest flight ever

above and left
Selection of Bryan's works machines.

109

110

111

109 Bryan's auto works – William Edward Bryan, George's father, on the left with a lorry load of his famous "Clock" amusements. The staff are pictured outside the works in Kegworth in 1934, but sadly it all burnt down in 1936 by a flash fire caused by cellulose paint spraying. The move to the new factory followed until it was closed at the outbreak of the 2nd World War.

110 Some of Bryan's works machines.

111 Bryan's garage Kegworth 1921/22. Bob Randon, pictured on the pumps, worked for W E Bryan until c.1970, at least 50 years' service. The young George Bryan worked for his father from the age of 16 to 19, from 1936 when the garage was re-built, to early 1940. The vintage car ride at Drayton Manor Theme Park has a station modelled on Colin's grandfather's garage.

112

112 Bryan's works exhibition stand at the Amusement Trades Exhibition at Horticultural Hall 1948. Jim Bryan left, Frank Thirkettle right.

undertaken by an airship. And he was presented with the Distinguished Flying Cross (DFC) for gallantry whilst on anti-submarine patrol – one of only four such medals to be awarded during World War I.

My father was teetotal – but he sometimes took with him a silver hip-flask containing brandy. Purely for medicinal purposes. Cockpits were open to the skies in those days and it was freezing cold!

After the war, my father opened up his own garage in Kegworth, Leicestershire. But he wasn't content with just that so he started a general engineering works as well as an electrical installation business. Highly innovative, he came up with the revolutionary idea of marketing a coin-operated petrol pump – and over 1,000 were sold before the Weights & Measures authorities frowned upon the idea, for reasons best known to themselves, and manufacturing ceased. I suppose you could say it was the forerunner of today's self-service petrol pump.

However, by the end of the 1920s, William E Bryan had taken out a number of patents for coin slot machines, including his very first, The Odd Clod, which had slots for a penny and a halfpenny. Customers at his garage soon found they could put their odd pennies to good use!

In 1930, after opening a factory at the rear of his garage, he produced The Clock, the machine that put Bryan's Works on the road to success. Players would put 1d in the machine, spin the hands on the dial, and hoped they would win a pay-out of anything between 2d and 2s.

Showmen couldn't get enough of them. Seaside pier arcades up and down the country were full of them. After all, they looked nothing like the "fruit machines" that would come along later, and the authorities were less likely to be bothered by them! The Clock, however, was only one of a complete range of machines invented by my father at that time. But I wonder how many people today can remember The Rippler, Payramid, All-Square or the Walden Goliath Crane? And what about the Automatic Peep Show, that was marketed in 1936? It probably wouldn't be allowed today, but almost 70 years ago, for the price of 1d you could peer into a machine – and look at a colony of live ants! Not quite "What the Butler Saw," but nevertheless thousands of people found it fascinating to take a look at the micro-world of the ant.

Sadly, in 1936, a flash-fire destroyed the workshop, but, fortunately, my father had had the foresight to previously acquire vacant factory premises in Kegworth, and production was switched there instead. My father rebuilt the garage and I ran that until I joined the Army in 1940.

The company was on the crest of a wave, when, war broke out again. My father closed his production factory on September 4, 1939 – and William E Bryan went back into uniform. He was demobbed in 1945 with the rank of Squadron Leader. But there were no handouts then to get you back on your feet again. No grants or financial assistance. I know it rankled my father to think that after risking his life in two world

113

BRYANS BREEZY TOYS

The range of toys pictured above are working models which perform in a life-like and entertaining manner when exposed to a wind—or draught from a fan.

They are Engineer designed, strongly and well constructed, brightly coloured and they appeal to all ages.

These Wind Driven Toys are also available in larger sizes for display and advertising purposes.

Patents and Designs are applied for. Copyrights and rights to alter the design or construction are reserved.

114

113 Colour drawings of Breezy Toys.

114 William Edward Bryan at the Bryan's works in Kegworth.

115
Bryan's 1920s garage prior to demolition.

wars – like so many other men – he could not get any help to restart his enterprise.

It took my father two years to get back into the amusement business, assisted by my younger brother Jim, who, following the death of my father in 1984, ran Bryan's Works until his own death in December 2003. Jim was three years younger than me and served two years National Service with the RAF in Aden. He wanted to be a pilot but because he had broken his arm in a cycling accident and suffered from a lack of mobility he had to settle for joining the ground staff instead. It was not what he really wanted but there was nothing he could do about it.

Jim, however, had kept the family business going throughout the war and after he had served his time in the RAF he took an ever-increasing role in the running of the family concern. He worked hand-in-glove with our father to create a business whose name, I am proud to say, is still revered today.

It was three years after the end of hostilities, in 1948, that my father took part in the Amusement Trades' Exhibition, introducing what many in the industry regarded as his finest-ever machines – the Disappearing Disc and the Magic String Cutter. For the price of 1d, a player could see a coin "disappear" before his very eyes. Or he could see a piece of string cut in two and then, by some "mystical" process, see the two pieces become one again.

The 50s saw a succession of other machines on the market, including the coin-operated rocking horse.

Apart from inventing, designing, manufacturing and supplying his coin operated amusement machines, my father also introduced a range of wind-driven toys, marketed as Bryan's Breezy Toys, which were popular with children of all ages.

It was, I suppose, an era of simple pleasures – when most families could only afford a game of bingo or to play their hand on the 1d fruit machines at the end of the seaside pier or the street-corner amusement arcade. Such machines – largely made redundant by the introduction of electronic equipment and advancements in hi-tech games – are now truly museum pieces, although, it has to be said, many are still in use in arcades up and down the country. In the museum at Drayton Manor, however, we have developed quite a collection of the slot machines and visitors can still try their hand on them. Bryan's machines were famous for their originality and production excellence and I am delighted that the tangible efforts of my father's lifetime work are now regarded and revered as collector's items.

I believe our museum provides a wonderful insight into a period in people's lives when the pursuit of pleasure was so much more unsophisticated than today. I know it is a source of great interest to not only the grandparents of today, who have many childhood memories of such amusement machines, but also their own grandchildren, who seem quite happy to turn off their Game Boys in order to spend a few minutes playing the slot machines! (We still have the 'old' pennies to use in them).

Long may it be so.

DRAYTON MANOR
ZOO
15p
DRAYTON MANOR
PARK AND ZOO
A DAYS ADVENTURE!
Nr. TAMWORTH, STAFFS. Tel. Tamworth 287979
160 ACRES OF PARKLAND, LAKES, ZOO AND ENTERTAINMENT
ZOO

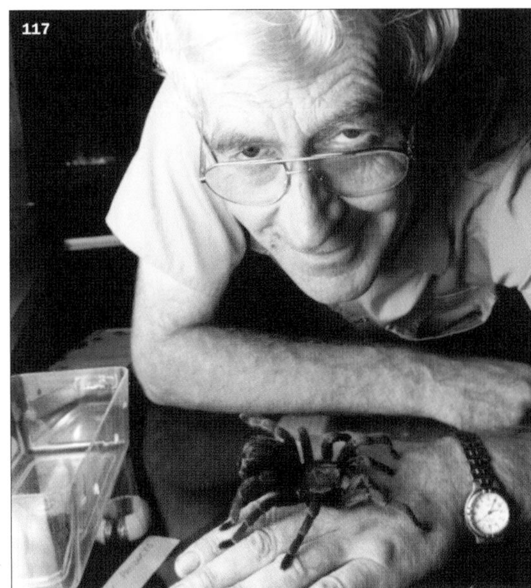

Chapter Six

Animal Magic

THE ZOO at Drayton Manor has been a popular attraction with visitors ever since it first opened, though zoos generally, because of changes in the views and attitudes of the public, do not now have the same widespread appeal compared to their heyday. I must admit that some zoos were terrible – and thankfully they have closed down.

Why do we keep ours going? Well, basically, because visitors continue to support it and come to see it. It is educational, of course. But it is also of tremendous interest, especially to little children, who find it a wonderful place to visit. Tastes change, I know, and I don't think that older children and teenagers have the same interest in the zoo as the toddlers do, but while it's an attraction we will continue to keep it open.

Ours covers 15-acres of the park and today it is home to a well-cared for collection of more than 100 different species from around the globe, who are looked after by dedicated, qualified and experienced handlers. All in all, we have everything from monkeys and birds of prey to big cats and reptiles. The Reptile House is home to one of Britain's largest groups of snakes and in John Foden, who was curator at the zoo for around 20 years, we were privileged to have as part of our team one of the world's leading herpetologists. In fact, we were honoured in October 2005 to host the annual conference of the Federation of British Herpetologists at Drayton Manor when leading experts, including Mark O'Shea, presenter of the popular "Big Adventure" TV series, paid a special tribute to the life and work of John Foden, who, sadly, died in 2000 aged just 52.

On his web-site, Mark also acknowledges their friendship over the years and recalls meeting John for the first time when he took a sick pet snake to him, seeking advice. "He gave me and my snake far more time out of his busy schedule than I am sure he could really afford. John became a good friend and whenever I am asked for advice by youngsters I always think back to the help he gave to me and try to pass on that enthusiasm."

John was, in fact, a good friend to many and it was most fitting that after his death, which followed a two year battle against cancer, several hundred people attended his funeral service, held at St Peter's Church, Drayton Bassett on March 14, 2000.

During his career, John also worked at Dudley Zoo, wrote a number of books on herpetology, and acted as advisor to a number of TV programmes. He was a founder member of the International Herpetological Society and acted as a consultant at Birmingham International and Heathrow Airports, working with Customs & Excise officials to rescue rare endangered species which were illegally imported into Britain. As an expert in his field (John was the first person in the country to breed golden pythons in captivity), he was also at the forefront of providing snake serum to hospitals and indeed helped to start a serum bank at the Liverpool School of Tropical Medicine to combat the effects of snake bits.

However, when you spend a lifetime working with venomous snakes I suppose it is almost inevitable that one day you will be bitten yourself and I recall one

116 & 117
John Foden,
zoo manager who
worked at Drayton
Manor for 30 years.

118 - 120
Zoo enclosures, cages, aviaries and walkways from the early days, late 1950s.

occasion when that actually happened to John. After being bitten, John cut his own wrist, calmly walked to the office and phoned for medical attention. And then the drama really started. For the serum that was needed for John's injection was in London and it had to be flown by Phantom Jet to Birmingham before being driven under police escort to Drayton Manor! Fortunately, John lived to tell the tale.

I suppose man has always had a certain fascination for reptiles and our visitors are no different. But amongst the most popular animals at the zoo are undoubtedly the chimps – some of which have been here over 40 years. But equally as delightful are our cotton-top Tamarins – miniature monkeys that are native to the tropical forests of Columbia. Maybe they are just too appealing – for in February 2005 thieves broke in and snatched a family of Tamarins from their cage. Fortunately, Staffordshire police recovered them the following day and there were tears of joy when Rio, Pinky and Baby were reunited with the zoo's primate keeper, Emma Swaddle.

The zoo originally started in 1957. We were receiving numerous visits by parties of schoolchildren during the week – but the "powers that be" were taking the view that if schools were to give their pupils a day out, then it had to be "educational." So that's how our zoo came into being. It opened in a relatively small way, our first animals being the monkeys, chimps and penguins which we housed in facilities which we constructed on an area of land close to our Garden Centre.

One of my great friends is Molly Badham and before she founded Twycross Zoo, together with Nat Evans, about 48 years ago, Molly used to bring along the chimps she had to Drayton Manor Zoo. Molly then had a pet shop at Sutton Coldfield and some land at Hints, near Tamworth, where she started to show her chimps. As everyone knows, the chimps were later

121 Llama and visitors.

122 Molly Badham with her Brooke Bond chimps performed in the Zoo on Sundays and Bank Holiday Mondays, pictured c.1959/60.

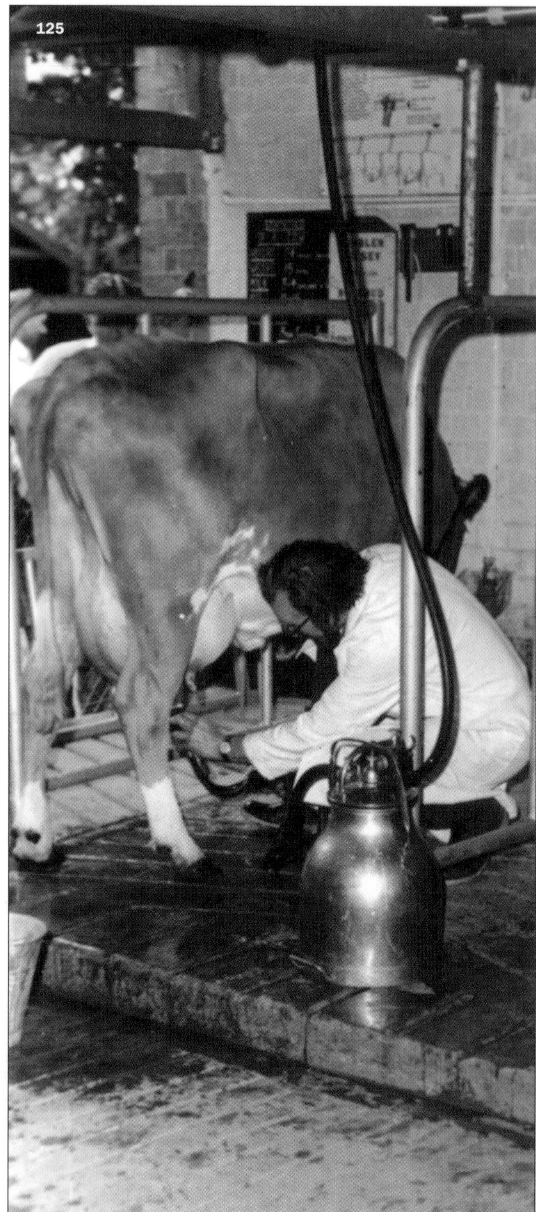

123
Molly Badham's Brooke Bond Chimps enjoying a picnic with photographer Garfield Snow's car in the background.

124 Molly Badham's chimp on bicycle.

125 Geoff Ingram milking a cow down on the Drayton Manor Farm

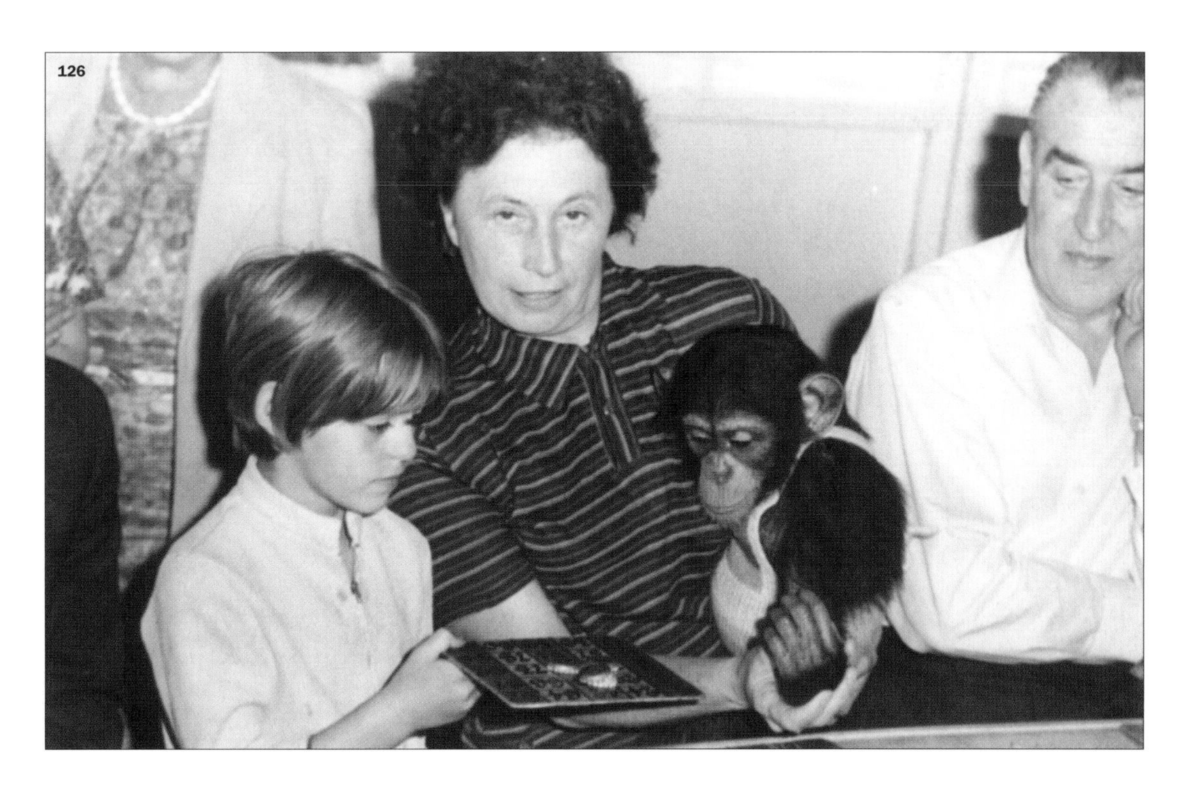

to become famous as the "stars" of the PG Tips television commercial.

At Drayton Manor, I erected a special stage for Molly – and her chimps used to perform before huge crowds. They were a massive attraction and never lost their popularity. However, Molly and Nat bought 40 acres of land at Twycross to open their own zoo, which was developed with the assistance of Geoff Ingram, my foreman at Drayton Manor, and his late wife, Joan.

It was a sad day for me when Geoff left to join Twycross Zoo but it was a career move he wanted to make and I never stood in his way. Geoff is still active today and our paths sometimes cross, giving us the opportunity to talk over old times.

Meanwhile, I had purchased additional land of my own – a nine acre plot adjacent to the park, which we developed as a Zoo Farm. The zoo continued to expand over 15 acres and we opened a Reptile House, introduced lions and a whole host of other animals and exotic birds. An artist even made life-size fibre-

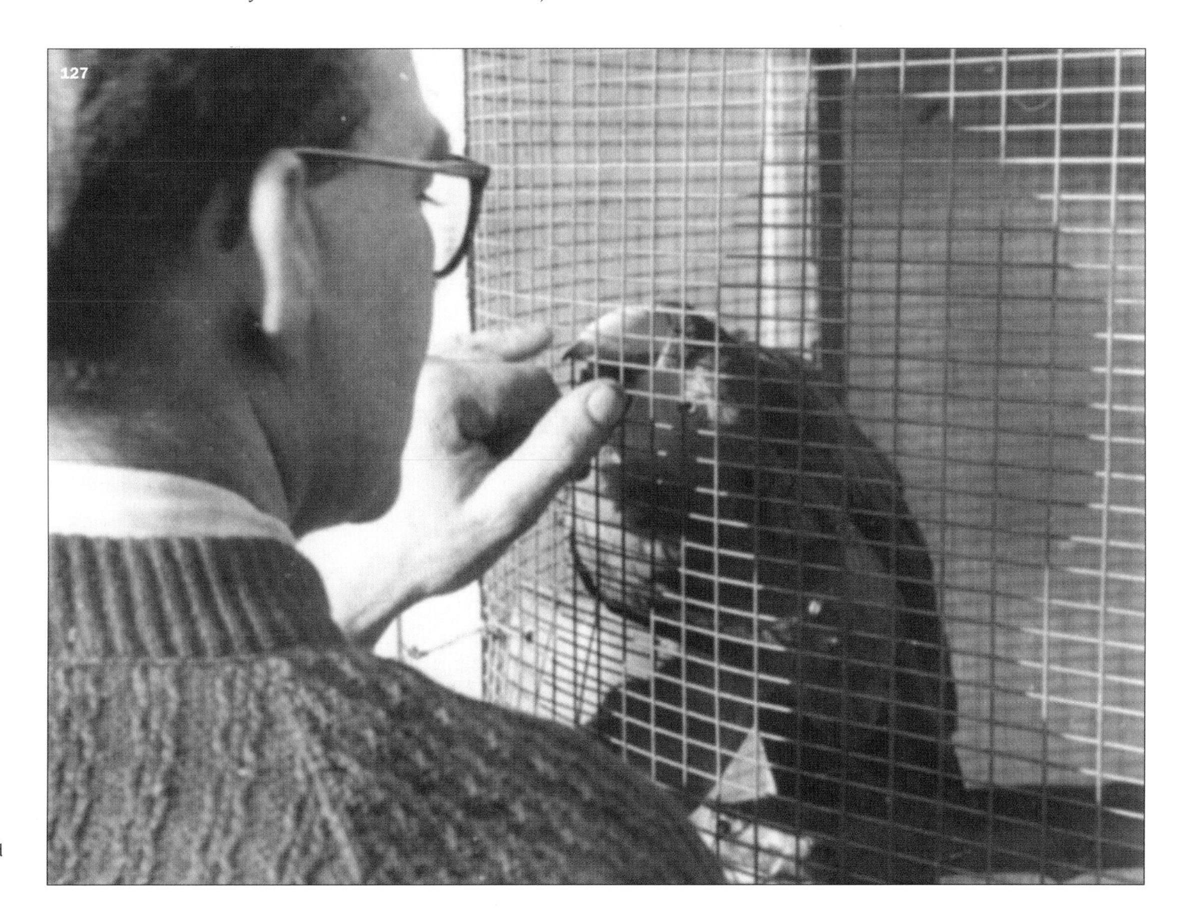

126 Joan Ingram with chimp playing bingo.

127 Geoff Ingram and parrot.

glass dinosaurs – and "The Lost World" feature is still as popular with today's youngsters as it was when it first appeared on the scene all those years ago.

It was during this period that I became a member of the Zoological Society. Being able to gain membership was particularly significant because at the time, those of us who were operating leisure establishments that involved attractions other than simply zoos were, quite frankly, frowned upon by the Zoo Federation. Especially stately homes such as Longleat and Woburn who opened safari parks within the grounds of their homes. Nowadays, of course, such attractions are big business. Not just in the UK but all over the world.

It was at this time that the government contemplated introducing a Parliamentary Act to licence zoos. Such a move was indeed welcome for it meant that poorly-kept zoos were closed. Naturally, the industry, wanted only the good ones to survive. Today, BIAZA, the British & Ireland Association of Zoos & Aquariums, and the British Association of Leisure Parks, Piers & Attractions (BALPPA) are the organisations which apply the rules. Operating licenses are much dearer than originally envisaged and although the zoo at Drayton Manor is itself a costly operation, we continue to maintain an all-inclusive admission charge.

It is a fact, however, that as the era of the "big ride" has increasingly captured the public's imagination, then numbers of visitors to the zoo have diminished. I don't think children over the age of eight are very interested. Youngsters have more pocket money today than previous generations and when they visit the park it is usually to experience the thrill of the rides. However, the zoo, and its learning centre, continues to appeal to "push-chair" children, their mums and grandparents, who genuinely appreciate being able to observe the mixed collection of animals.

Of course, trends and fashions are always changing. What's "in" one year is "out" the next. The trick to being successful is anticipating the changes and being able to plan accordingly, and knowing how to meet whatever problems there are.

The zoo at Drayton Manor, however, will remain, although it is no longer a major part of our activities. That does not mean that we do not pay attention to every detail of its operation. We are extremely proud of the zoo and its staff. And to see the sheer delight on the faces of younger children when they watch the antics of animals who originate from some far-off land is a source of great pleasure.

128
Zoo promotion in a local pet shop.

129 Vera Bryan with baby chimp at Molly Badham's.

130
Lord Lieutenant of Staffordshire James Hawley bestows the OBE on a proud George Bryan, Sept. 28th 2004.

131
George Bryan and Vera Bryan.

Chapter Seven

Giving something back

THE leisure industry has been a way of life for Vera and me for well over 60 years. But I am glad to say that it has not dominated our lives to the exclusion of everything else.

On the contrary, we have been fortunate in that our work at Drayton Manor has helped us to forge strong, long-lasting links with the community at large. Links which culminated in one of the proudest days of my life – being awarded the OBE in 2004 for services rendered to tourism. It was certainly an unforgettable experience when, accompanied by my wife, I received the award from the Lord Lieutenant of Staffordshire, James Hawley, in a ceremony at the County Building, Stafford. I considered it a most fitting location to receive the honour – indeed, I will always be indebted to Staffordshire for everything that it has given Vera and myself; enduring friendships, a family to be proud of, business opportunities and a chance to serve the community.

Two years after we moved to Drayton Manor, I joined Tamworth Round Table and Vera became a member of the Ladies Circle. It was a wonderful introduction to the area and friends we made then are still amongst our best friends today. When I reached the age of 40, in 1961, I joined Rotary and I am still involved even now, as is my wife in the ladies organisation, the Inner Wheel. I became President in 1969 – and helped conceive the idea of an annual Kids Day Out at Drayton Manor. It happens on the first Wednesday in June when 500 Rotarians from the entire District – that's 68 Rotary Clubs – give up their day to entertain 1,500 disadvantaged children. I can't emphasis enough just how wonderful a day that is – for everyone concerned. To me, it also brings home the significance of Rotary's motto – Service Above Self.

In 1969, service to the community took me in another direction as well. I was asked to go on a Hospital Management Committee, because of my business aptitude, to act as a lay manager for hospitals in Tamworth, Lichfield, Sutton Coldfield and Erdington. I served on the committee for four years and during this time I developed a very strong interest in the mental health sector which, ultimately, saw me helping to form a new type of "watch-dog" group, known as Community Health Councils.

I was elected as CHC chairman and through that role met the Rev Paul Brothwell of Whittington Church. One day, he told me that his vicarage was going up for sale. He said he wished there was some way in which the property could be converted into a hospice.

It was an idea that eventually became reality – and I am delighted to be able to say that I was one of a seven-strong group which helped found what is now St Giles Hospice. I remain a vice-president of the hospice to this day, and although I am not as heavily involved with the organisation as I once was, I have the utmost regard and admiration for those who work there, dedicating themselves to those whose lives are, unfortunately, affected by cancer. And it was with great pride that I hosted a special ceremony at Drayton Manor in 2004 when the Lord Lieutenant

presented the Queen's Award for Voluntary Service to St Giles Hospice volunteers.

Later, I was asked to serve on the Burton-on-Trent based South East Staffordshire Health Authority. It was an onerous task, one which involved my attendance at monthly meetings. But it was most rewarding – and it gave me another opportunity to get involved with mental health, this time at the huge mental hospital at Burntwood, near Lichfield. My health duties also saw me serving on the Premier Health Committee, which gave me an involvement with the new Sir Robert Peel Hospital at Tamworth.

I spent many years serving on hospital committees – and at times I was less than appreciative of the way the particular government of the day was acting! A total of 136 mental hospitals were demolished and thousands of beds were lost without any provision being made for the people suffering from mental health problems. Community care is all well and good and the "salt of the earth" mental health nurses try their best, but how can they make up for short-sighted government decisions?

I can't tell you how astounded I was when, in 1985, the 28-bedded mental wing at the new Sir Robert Peel Hospital was named after me. But what an honour it was for Vera and me when I was called upon to officially open the facility. It's a proud moment that will last in our memories for ever.

I continued being a director until 1995 and a member of the Premier Health Committee until it was disbanded. But I was 75 years old then, so I wasn't complaining! Belonging to such committees, however, and serving alongside other business-focused members, who were also freely giving of their time and expertise, was an enriching experience I would not have missed. I was also aged 75 when I retired from being a Tax Commissioner of Offlow North– a duty I had performed for 21 years. This involved sitting on a tribunal once a month at Burton, Tamworth or Lichfield and helping taxpayers solve

opposite
Charity balloon launch with George Bryan's daughter, Jane, pictured on the left.

132, 133 & 134
Rotary Kids Out 2005 when over 2000 children enjoyed a special day out to remember.

135 The George Bryan Mental Health Centre, 1995.

136 Newly furnished Mental Health Unit at George Bryan Centre. Pictured are Martin Dunkley, locality director, Mrs Vera Bryan, George Bryan, Cllr Margaret Whalley and Margaret Stanhope, chairman of South Staffs Health Authority.

137 St Giles Hospice. Picture shows George Bryan and Appeal Committee Chairman, Peter Brown OBE and fundraiser for St Giles, George Briffett.

138 HRH Queen Elizabeth II inspects the new RNLI lifeboat, 'Drayton Manor'.

139 Vera Bryan, Helen and Daisy Pawley at the RNLI day.

140 Colin Bryan pictured with the RNLI crew from Blackpool.

whatever differences they had with the Inland Revenue over tax payments. This was very worthwhile, for it was all about helping real people with real problems.

Vera, on the other hand, has also kept herself very busy, undertaking significant charity work, with the Royal National Lifeboat Institute (RNLI) being one of the organisations nearest and dearest to her heart. I suppose it goes back all those years to when Vera, as a child, stood with a collecting box, cajoling the public to give a few pence in order to support the lifeboat men!

Today, visitors to Drayton Manor are also helping to fund-raise for the RNLI. In fact, they have been doing so for a number of years, ever since our son Colin, Drayton Manor's chief executive, negotiated with the RNLI an agreement so that they would receive 1p every time someone took a ride on Stormforce 10, one of our most popular attractions.

In 2004, when Vera was 86, there was an occasion we will always remember. She helped "launch" the "Drayton Manor Lifeboat" in a ceremony at the park – the culmination of a fund-raising exercise in which we, and visitors, raised a grand total of £75,000. Because the lifeboat was made of rubber, however, Vera couldn't break a bottle of champagne over its bows – so she had to pour the bubbly over the vessel instead!

144

Jumbo Jet

WAY IN

Chapter Eight

Era of the big rides

141 The Mississippi Show boat had a Fun House inside, 1985.

142 A Pinfari ZL42 Coaster, The Python, one of the first coasters at Drayton Manor opened in 1985.

143 The Balloon Race 1987.

144 Jumbo City Jet 1, a Shwarzkopf ride, the first coaster at Drayton Manor, before the Pinfari ZL42 looping coaster.

145 The Paratower installed in 1982, one of only 4 in the world.

146 The Pirate Ship 1982.

147 The Flying Dutchman with the Paratower in the background, with Managing Director Colin Bryan, June 1983.

148 & 149 Apocalypse

DRAYTON MANOR has come a long way since its official opening in 1950. We have been transported into another era – spirited away by the Big Rides, whose magnetic appeal attracts legions of thrill-seekers from all over the country. Today, as the fifth most visited theme park in the UK, and proud winner of awards such as the Best UK Attraction for Children (an honour we received in 2003, 2004 and 2005), we have the capacity to accommodate up to 20,000 people per hour on breath-taking rides such as Shockwave, Stormforce 10 and Apocalypse, the world's first stand-up tower drop, which first opened in 2000.

My son-in-law Richard Pawley, then Operations Director at Drayton Manor, worked with Swiss designers to create the awesome Apocalypse, which set new world standards in theme park technology – and which offers riders a terrifying 50 mph (80kmph) drop from a height of over 180ft (54m)! For those of you who haven't yet had the "pleasure" of experiencing Apocalypse, let me tell you that passengers can either sit or stand – before being tilted forward at an agonising angle of 15 degrees from vertical, then hoisted skywards, stranded on a two-tonne launch shuttle. Next, they feel the rush of a devastating drop with nothing to stop them but a powerful magnetic field. And it is quite literally breath-taking, for riders experience a test pilot 4+G as the ground rushes towards them. One side of the tower is fitted with a unique stand-up shuttle. There's no footrest at all – and riders hang from 180 ft up with nothing to hold them but their over-the-shoulder restraints. It's absolutely floorless! But why not try it for yourself and see what you think?

Our first major ride, the Chairlift, opened in 1964. Today, it's still very much a popular attraction – and its installation heralded the start of an expansion phase which, by the 80s, had witnessed a doubling in size of Drayton Manor. In fact, we have introduced a new, or updated, ride every year since 1981. Between 1990-2005 our investment was in excess of £30 million. And that's not counting the £800,000 we spend annually on essential maintenance.

Sadly, however, the Chairlift, which was manufactured by a company named British Chairlifts, is the

150 Octopus with MD Colin Bryan (second from left) July 1985.

151 & 152 Stormforce 10.

153 & 154 Reverchon Log Flume, modified 1986/87.

155 MD Colin Bryan with PR consultant Helen O'Neill on Shockwave.

only UK-made ride, apart from the smaller ones, that still operates at Drayton Manor today. The Americans, Swiss, French, Italians, Dutch and Germans have all manufactured the Big Rides – not us. I just cannot understand why we haven't entered the market; after all, practically every country in the world now wants them. But, there again, I am not the only one to express sorrow at the demise of manufacturing in the UK.

Our first proper white-knuckle theme park ride – the log flume – was built in 1981. We upgraded it over the years but eventually replaced it in 1999 with the more exciting Stormforce 10 – a wet knuckle ride and the country's first reverse chute water coaster, which plunges down three spectacular drops (the last one being 16 metres) along its 500 metre long track.

Constructed at a cost of £3 million, the ride won a top leisure industry award as Best New European Attraction. Based on a Cornish fishing village, the ride is centred around a lifeboat rescue, with its eight themed cars being launched in true lifeboat style. Stormforce 10 takes just four minutes to complete– during which time it pulls 3+G and has a maximum speed of 40 mph –and at peak times it handles 1,500 passengers an hour. It is also the first ride in the world to be associated with a registered charity – the Royal National Lifeboat Institution. And I am delighted to say that by donating 1p for every passenger that uses Stormforce 10 – and 25p every time they buy their own "action-replay" photograph – Drayton Manor has been able to raise sufficient funds to buy a brand new Atlantic 75 inshore lifeboat for the RNLI. It was ceremoniously handed over in 2004.

It was 1994, however, that turned out to be a milestone year. That was when we launched the £4.2 million Shockwave, Europe's only stand-up roller coaster. It was an instant success – and has been ever since, each season attracting over one million enthusiasts who never seem to mind queuing in order to relish a unique mind-blowing experience. From a dizzy height of 120ft, Shockwave swirls its passengers around through nearly four times the force of gravity in a series of loops, corkscrews and turns. It's daring, different – and the darling of the Roller Coaster Club of Great Britain, which voted it the Best Stand-Up Roller Coaster in the World. We also have another water ride – Splash Canyon, which, as well as whirls and rapids, features special-effects machines to create waves and fog.

Two years later, in 1996, we introduced The Haunting, the first public participation ride of its kind in any theme park in the UK and then we unveiled the

above
Shockwave – Europe's only stand up roller coaster.

156 Splash Canyon.

157 & 158 The Jungle Cruise, 1976 to 2002, was transformed into Excalibur. Jungle Cruise was designed by Alan Hawes, after George and Vera's visit to Disney World.

159
Colin Bryan with Group Leisure Award, Best UK Attraction for Children which the park won 3 years in a row – 2003, 4 and 5.

160 Young Edward Pawley and William Bryan at the launch of the Sky Flyer by Dr Who, alias Jon Pertwee.

161 Andi Peters launching The Haunting in 1996.

Magnificent Seven – seven new rides for the '98 summer season.

We waved the '90s goodbye by introducing the £3 million Stormforce 10 and invested a further £2 million to welcome in the new Millennium with Apocalypse.

In 2004, it was Pandemonium! That's the name of the ride where the world turns upside down for 64 thrill-seekers positioned in two 32-seater platforms, which swing simultaneously through 360 degrees to a height of almost 25 metres. Experiencing a force of 3.8G, passengers fleetingly pass each other as they fly in circles through the air! It's not for me – but thousands of visitors can't get enough of it. And, once you have been on it, how can you ever forget the stomach-churning Maelstrom, Europe's only gyro swing?

Our latest Big Ride, the £3 million G Force, was launched in the summer of 2005, appropriately enough, by chart-topping "popera" group, G4, the members of which, Jon Ansell, Matt Stiff, Michael Christie and Ben Thepa, delighted the crowds with a rendition of "My Way" before becoming the first people to brave the new-look ride.

It's the only one of its kind in the world. It shoots you upwards, backwards and onwards – and is guaranteed to get everyone screaming!

Hailed as revolutionary by the world's theme park and roller coaster aficionados, G4 features seats which have a completely new hip-restraint system. Ideal for incredible inversions, the new seats in the ride's X cars leave passengers hanging from the hip, dangling totally free to experience the ride of their life. Each six-seater car also features a unique Big Boy seat – specially designed to carry riders who may otherwise be unable to enjoy roller coasters due to their size.

G Force is the first ride in the UK to include such a feature, offering white-knuckle excitement to riders who are of a larger frame or especially tall. And its two cars also have stadium seating – with each pair seated higher than the one in front, offering all riders a

above
G Force with G4 at the official launch, July 2005.

terrifying view of the action!

As popular as they are, however, Drayton Manor is not just about Big Rides. There are less scary attractions, which enable us to offer the perfect mix – catering for both families and thrill seekers.

For instance, there is the Jolly Roger family boat ride, which sits alongside the Jolly Buccaneer and Pirate Adventure features in the themed Pirate Cove area of the 280-acre park. The Pirate Adventure indoor boat ride is similar to Disney's Pirates of the Caribbean – and is a good way to relax after

162 Klondike Old Mine opened in 1995, replaced by G Force in 2005.

163–165 Pirate Adventure launch of July 19th 1990. Construction shot with scaffolding. Launch shots (l-r) Colin Bryan, Managing Director, Richard Pawley who was Project Director for the ride, George Bryan (centre) and TV personality, Timmy Mallett, and staff dressed as pirates.

Shockwave! Enthusiasts rate it as one of the best rides of its kind in the UK, with visitors being taken on a seven seas journey which whisks them into pirate town and a battle on the high seas!

And there is also the captivating, family-orientated ride, Excalibur – a Dragon's Tale, which girl band Atomic Kitten officially opened in 2003. This is where 15 boats, each carrying up to 12 passengers, "transport" visitors back in time to King Arthur's Ancient Kingdom, where they witness 14 action-packed scenes of legendary lands and knights of old. All made possible, of course, through state-of-the-art technology!

At peak times, 2,400 people pass through the gates of Drayton Manor every hour and, on average, people spend anything up to six hours at the park, enjoying our 100 rides and other attractions, such as the 350-seater theatre that is the venue for our circus. A circus without animals, that is, and one that instead features entertainers such as acrobats, jugglers and clowns. Our first theatre-style event, however, was the Jungle Palladium – a puppet show that captivated everyone.

I like to think Drayton Manor's popularity is constant because it appeals to the whole family – from youngsters to grandparents. However, we are not complacent and we realise we can never afford to rest on our laurels. That's why we are always having to plan several years ahead – doing our best to crystal-gaze and predict future trends in the leisure industry.

Celebrity guests

Here pictured are just a few of the many celebrities who have enjoyed a visit to Drayton Manor.

top left & **top right** Blue Peter's Chris Trace opens the model railway..

centre left B*witched launch Apocalypse.

centre right Mrs Lynne Bryan and Colin Bryan with Tommy Boyd who opened the Reptile House in 1992.

above left John Noakes opens the Jungle Cruise in July 1976. Sitting on the table is William Bryan and Edward Pawley, with little George Bryan Jnr waiting for an autograph.

above Gabrielle Drake, husband Louis De Wet and Julie Miller from Drayton Manor zoo.

left Noel Edmonds with Colin Bryan opens the river rapids ride Splash Canyon.

above Steps get wet at the opening of Stormforce 10.

top right Hear'say launch Maelstrom.

right Atomic Kitten and Excalibur swords and boats.

below G4 ride on G Force at the official launch, July 2005.

167
166
Your Affectionate Nephew
W. E. Bryan
20·12·15
169
168
THE YEAR OF THE
ROLLER COASTER
94
170
DRAYTON MANOR PARK
INLAND
PLEASURE RESORT
PARTY & CASUAL
CATERING
DRAYTON
MANOR
PARK

166 William Edward Bryan in 1915.

167 Holiday shot of Vera and George in deckchairs with their young son, Colin, and Max the dog, taken on their last holiday just before they moved to Drayton Manor in 1949. They used William Edward Bryan's caravan - his Caravan Club membership number was No.1!

168 Celebrating the Year of the Roller Coaster in 1994, taken at the Park Lane Hilton, London (left to right) William Bryan, Colin Bryan, Edward Pawley.

169 Dragon kiddie coaster 1990 George Bryan, Colin Bryan, Richard Pawley.

170 Drayton Manor Inland Pleasure Resort: Vera and George Bryan with their children Colin, Jane and Andrew and friend Sheila Morrison

171 Front row: Jane Pawley, George Bryan OBE, Vera Bryan, Colin Bryan, Back row: Lynne Bryan, William Bryan, Richard Pawley, Edward Pawley, George Bryan, Helen Pawley.

172 (l-r) standing, Andrew Bryan, George Bryan, Colin Bryan with Jane Pawley (née Bryan) and their mother, Vera.

Chapter Nine

A dynasty of family fun

DRAYTON MANOR is a family business in every sense of the word.

Three generations of the Bryan family are running the theme park and we are united in a common objective – to bring fun and laughter to the lives of the thousands of families who visit our location each year.

Today, I am chairman of the organisation, having handed over my role as chief executive to my son, Colin, in 1987. But that does not mean to say I have simply become a "figurehead." At the age of 84 I still go to the office every working day, although, naturally, all day-to-day responsibility and future planning is in the hands of Colin.

Getting to the office every day isn't as arduous as you might imagine. Vera and I live within the grounds of the 280-acre park and we have done so for well over half a century, occupying a former Peel estate cottage, which we have extended over the years! We have spent many a happy holiday around the world, but I can't imagine a more perfect spot to live than our own countryside setting.

Colin and his wife, Lynne, live nearby and it was in his home that we received Princess Anne, now the Princess Royal, when she visited Drayton Manor in 1998. She is a most gracious person and displayed a genuine interest in the park and its history, especially its links with Sir Robert Peel and Queen Victoria.

Our other son, Andrew, who lives in Wales, decided early on in his career that the theme park business was not for him. However, as head of the management side of the company's hotel division, he is also carrying on the family business. In the early 70s, Andrew went off to London and for 14 years he enjoyed a role in the movie industry, working for Warner Films and meeting top stars such as Clint Eastwood. When the time came for a career change, Andrew moved to Wales, becoming a director of our hotel division and completing an acquisition in the Brecon Beacons – that of the Tynewydd Country Hotel, a 29-bedroom facility for banqueting, set in a most delightful rural location. Today, it is one of three hotels which we currently operate within the division.

173 Andrew Bryan on the Buffalo coaster.

174 Colin's son George Bryan aged 18 and his MG Metro Turbo racing car in front of Shockwave, 1995.

175 William Edward Bryan at George and Vera's house.

176 General Manager William Bryan and Project Manager Edward Pawley 1994.

177 William Bryan at Disney World Florida where he was learning about the theme park industry.

178 Helen Pawley, Richard Pawley, Rachel Pawley and her husband Edward Pawley try out the Megafobia coaster at Oakwood, Pembrokeshire.

Although Jane, our daughter, did not originally join the business – preferring instead to bring up her own family – her husband, Richard Pawley did. Jane, however, is now our company secretary.

Richard, who, together with my son Colin was instrumental in creating the explosion of new rides at the park, remained with Drayton Manor for 27 years before branching out on his own. As operations director, he played an integral part in the development of Drayton Manor and was responsible for innovations in amusement rides such as the first reversible chute in the UK, the first free fall stand-up tower ride in the world and the first stand-up roller coaster in Europe. Today, as chief executive of his own company, Richard remains a leading figure in leisure development, having also held key positions in organisations such as the British Association of Leisure Parks, Piers and Attractions (BALPPA) and the International Association of Amusement Parks & Attractions.

Edward and Helen, Jane and Richard's children, are also very much part of our organisation.

Edward, who is currently Rides Projects Manager at Drayton Manor, studied at a school of tourism after completing his formal education. Then it was off to

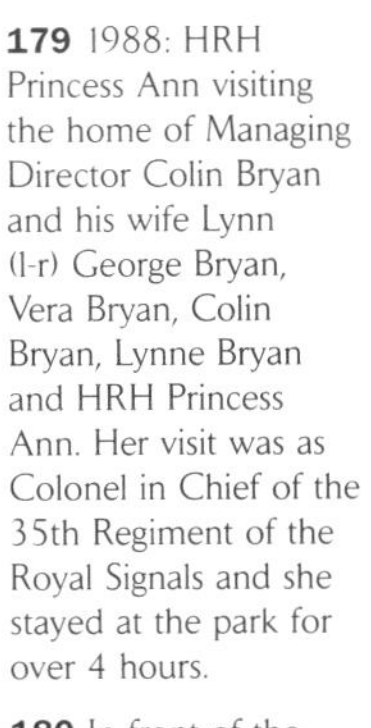

179 1988: HRH Princess Ann visiting the home of Managing Director Colin Bryan and his wife Lynn (l-r) George Bryan, Vera Bryan, Colin Bryan, Lynne Bryan and HRH Princess Ann. Her visit was as Colonel in Chief of the 35th Regiment of the Royal Signals and she stayed at the park for over 4 hours.

180 In front of the Drayton Manor Park sign:
Left to right: Chairman George Bryan OBE, General Manager William Bryan, Managing Director Colin Bryan MHCIMA, and then Director of Operations Richard Pawley.

find work experience – and what an experience it was, working in Belgium, Germany, then at Thorpe Park –the favourite theme park of the late Princess of Wales – and later running a park owned by the Sultan of Brunei for a whole year. I think Edward must have made rather a good impression in Brunei – for later we had six of the Sultan's wives and their entourage visit Drayton Manor for the day! They were holidaying in London at the time, but they must have read about the park – or seen something about us on an Internet website. So they all decided to drive to Tamworth for the day. The whole party thoroughly enjoyed their stay – especially when it came to the big rides and treating themselves to the food on offer in the restaurant!

181 Richard Pawley, Helen Pawley and Edward Pawley at the annual convention of the International Association of Amusement Parks and Attractions.

182 George and Vera Bryan at Drayton Manor.

183 George Bryan and Geoff Ingram 2005.

184 George and Vera at home celebrating her 80th birthday.

185 George and Vera outside The Haunting in 1996.

186 4 generations of the Bryan family – Colin, George, Ethan, George junior.

187 Colin, George, Andrew Bryan at the Tynewydd Country Hotel.

188 The family at the launch of Maelstrom with pop stars, Hear'say.

As for Helen, she attended the University of Birmingham for 3 years – and left with an honours degree in leisure management. Now she is employed at Drayton Manor as a manager engaged in HR, health & safety and guest relations duties.

George, Colin's son, has taken a shine to the world of gardening and horticulture. So, as our co-general manager, he is also playing an active role in the further development – and preservation – of the grounds of Drayton Manor as a major leisure "oasis." William – George's elder brother – is also co-general manager and, as such, is a key member of the team in whose hands lies the future of Drayton Manor. William was educated at Wylde Green College and Sutton College before going on to Birmingham Catering College. He also spent a year working at Disney World, where he gained valuable experience and amassed a tremendous knowledge of the leisure industry.

I like to think that the "building blocks" we put in place all those years ago have provided the foundation stones for a solid, reliable business enterprise. So where do we go in the future? What plans are there for the continued development of Drayton Manor? I think that's best answered in a subsequent chapter by my son, Colin, who has been chief executive of Drayton Manor since 1987.

price 4p
DRAYTON
MANOR
PARK AND ZOO
THE PLEASURE CENTRE OF THE MIDLANDS
Nr. TAMWORTH, STAFFS

Welcome to
Drayton
Manor Park & Zoo
Price 3p
THE PLEASURE CENTRE OF THE
MIDLANDS - NR. TAMWORTH - STAFFS

15p
DRAYTON
MANOR
PARK AND ZOO
A DAYS ADVENTURE!
Nr. TAMWORTH, STAFFS. Tel. Tamworth 287979
160 ACRES OF PARKLAND, LAKES, ZOO
AND ENTERTAINMENT

15p
Drayton
Manor
Park
Nr. TAMWORTH, STAFFS
Tel. Tamworth 287979
The
FAMILY
LEISURE
PARK
LEISURE
PARK and ZOO
160 ACRES OF
PARKLAND, LAKES,
ZOO AND
ENTERTAINMENT
DRAYTON MANO
PARK AND ZOO
Fazeley Nr Tamworth St

Christmas at
Drayton Manor
It's a great place to party

Chapter Ten

Summing up – from the 70s to today

LOOKING back over the years, I suppose the 1970s was a decade of great sadness – a time of loss of many Midland factories with famous names, the closure of coal mines, and a general run-down of the region's great industries. It was also a time which changed my thinking. In 1975, Vera and I went to America for three weeks, specifically to see the opening of Disney World in Florida. It was mind-boggling – especially to see the vastness of 33,000 acres of Florida scrub land which had been purchased by Walt Disney to prevent other interested leisure parties setting up nearby.

Vera and I wondered at the sheer magnificence of every building, the superb attractions, and the ingenuity of the whole project – it was a real shock to the system! We knew we could never achieve such a project at Drayton but we knew full well we needed to grow. And it was on the way home that I realised I would have to give great thought and consideration as to how we would move forward in the future.

Thankfully, our economy started to improve and the nation got back to some sort of normality after a truly disastrous period in our history. However, I just could not believe that no-one in our country was producing equipment for our "still new" type of business. It was a subject which I often used to discuss with our MP, Sir David Lightbown, who sadly died in 1995. Just why didn't Great Britain manufacture our type of equipment for theme and amusement parks? It was something I could never understand – and still don't to this day. Other countries manufactured the equipment then and still do now.

My first task upon our return from Disney was to build a Jungle Cruise on our 2.3 acre smaller lake. It was with good fortune that an American named Alan Hawes came to see me. He had worked in the US and had designed and built a Jungle Cruise there. And so, our own very excellent and unique ride was officially opened in 1976 by John Noakes from the BBC's Blue Peter children's programme. It was a great and successful ride which lasted until the construction of the Excalibur ride in 2003.

Then we decided to build a version of Disney's "Pirates of the Caribbean" indoor water ride. We named ours "The Pirate Adventure" and it marked our 40th year in business. It was opened on July 19, 1990, by Timmy Mallet and was then our largest project. Today, it is still today one of the biggest indoor water rides in the world and a firm favourite with our visitors.

The Pirate Adventure, incorporating 98 moving figures involved in many battle scenes, was a huge project, costing in excess of £3 million. But I am glad to say that son-in-law Richard, then working as the theme park's operations director, succeeded, together with the Golding family of Colchester and various subcontractors, in building and unveiling what was then our largest project. Today, it is still one of the biggest

opposite and above
a selection of advertising brochures from past and present.

attractions of its kind in the world and remains a firm favourite with our visitors.

Our learning curve in respect of the newer types of ride continued due to the ability of Richard, and that of my sons Colin and Andrew, to establish excellent working relationships with the foreign – mostly European – firms which were manufacturing the new generation of theme park rides. There were no British rides available of the size that we needed – and I know I have mentioned it before, but I am proud to be British and this lack of home-grown manufacturing is something that disappoints me even now.

We purchased our first Compact Coaster in 1981. It was a City Jet coaster made in 1976 by Anton Schwarzkopf of West Germany and we went to Holland to see it, where the ride had been set up in a town square. Three years later we replaced the City Jet with a new Zamperla ZL42 Zyclon looping coaster. Our first big Roller Coaster, Shockwave, which opened in 1994, was made by a Swiss firm, Intamin. It is still, after 12 years, the only stand-up coaster in Europe and is as good as any in the world. ACE (American Coaster Enthusiasts), the Rollercoaster Club of Great Britain and the European Coaster Club enthusiasts all say so, any way!

Stormforce 10, our new ride for our 50th season in 1999, was a replacement of the much loved Log Flume from 1981 to 1998. It was hugely popular, having the first eight-seater boats designed to look like RNLI sea rescue boats, the first reverse drop in the UK, and taking eight minutes to circumnavigate one route. The whole concept took Richard and Colin two years to design and I am pleased to say that it was mostly constructed by UK firms, including the Leicester-based firm Farmer Studios, who themed the ride to look like a scene in a dockyard in a very rough sea. This is one of the wettest water rides in the industry! The boats, pumps and mechanicals are, however, all manufactured in Switzerland. They do seem to make the long- lasting equipment which is needed with the continuous onslaught we have year in, year out.

Although we have German, Italian, Swiss, American and Dutch rides, design work is carried out much closer to home. Mark Golding of Colchester (Space Leisure) is at the forefront of his profession. He is a superb designer, not only theming rides but also preparing plans and designs of theme park buildings. Another top man is Ken Rundle, a master of refurbishment who restores equipment to as-good-as-new condition. He also manufactured rides to order, including the ever-popular Gallopers.

189 Staff party 1975 for the park's 25th anniversary.

190 Staff outside the Tower Tearoom c.1965.

191 Young Michael Pawliw on the landing craft; he was a Pole who came up from California in England and then went to work at Foseco next door, as an industrial chemist.

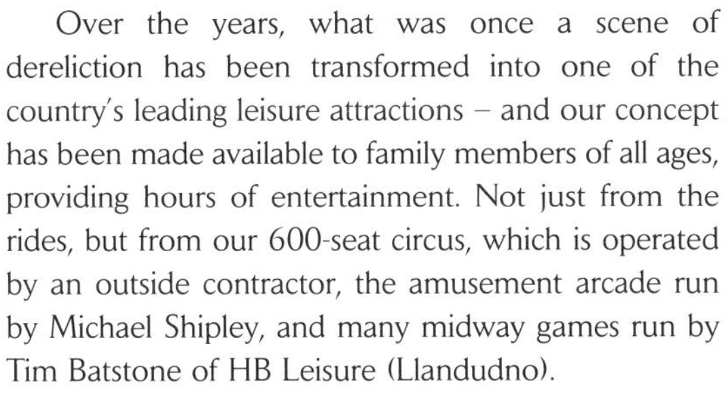

Over the years, what was once a scene of dereliction has been transformed into one of the country's leading leisure attractions – and our concept has been made available to family members of all ages, providing hours of entertainment. Not just from the rides, but from our 600-seat circus, which is operated by an outside contractor, the amusement arcade run by Michael Shipley, and many midway games run by Tim Batstone of HB Leisure (Llandudno).

I am truly delighted that the enterprise started by Vera and myself continues to grow under the direction of my son, Colin, with other members of the family – grandchildren William and George Bryan, Edward and Helen Pawley - being key members of the team. We are a proud family business. Our other son, Andrew, who together with his wife Catherine has given us our fifth and sixth grandchildren – Andrew and Millicent – is now operating three Drayton Manor Hotels in Wales.

I feel I must also mention the many excellent sub-contractors who, over the years, have responded with excellent work and first class knowledge of the many different facets of our business. Harry Price was the most brilliant plasterer and tile layer, Ron Twomlow and his company are wonderful joiners – the excellence of their work is still on view today, and Derek and his son Jonathan Pope have done most of our in-house décor. Alan Grieveson and his men were here 35 years - tarmac roads and other big projects being testimony to his skills.

Then there's Neil Beniston of DF Beniston of Pype Hayes, our builder who, with all of his excellent work, has transformed the outlook of our new themed buildings. Ian Hamer of Spanclad, Bromsgrove, has designed and erected most of the steelwork in all the very large indoor rides buildings. And Keith Price of Hereford, a knowledgeable steeple jack and his team, who are now erecting major rides all over Europe, benefiting from their experience here.

All have been with us over many years, always showing the high standards of excellence we demand and maintaining a sense of responsibility to the public, who use and enjoy the facilities provided. There is no doubt about it, we are proud of our appearance, cleanliness, and fair charges which bring our guests in again and again.

There has never been a dull day in all our time at Drayton Manor. And I regard it as a privilege whenever I see the joy on the face of a visitor running to try out a new ride for that every first time.

Not only do we thank our many patrons, we most sincerely thank and respect our local employees and those from elsewhere for their consistent pleasantness and loyal assistance to our customers.

192 George Bryan with Mr and Mrs Hunt at the toy shop c.1953/1954.

193 Presentation of watches for 21 years' service.
Back row (standing l-r) Mrs Timpson, Mrs Jordan, Sid Harris, John Price, Mrs Somers, Mrs Starkey.
Front row (sitting l-r) Alma Dick, Vera Bryan, George Bryan, Mrs Keast.

194 Young Michael Liquorish worked on the Crazy Golf.

195 The 100 year old carousel was restored by Keith Donaldson and Bill Harding (pictured).

World Class
Thrills
Drayton Manor
THEME PARK
SHOCKWAVE
animal
magic

Erin
Ben
Pam
Fred
Tina
Eric
UK Attraction
the best
for Children
DUMPY
fun
for all the family

Drayton Manor Theme Park – c.1954

Drayton Manor Theme Park – c.1962

An aerial shot of Drayton Manor Theme Park taken in August 2002

Chapter Eleven

Future plans

by Colin Bryan

FOR the last ten years, I have had a vision of what a "new" Drayton Manor could look like in the future. Now I am hoping it will not be too much longer before that vision becomes reality.

Today, the leisure industry is not one to stand still – just look at the way investment continues to pour into the sector, now worth £60+ billion in the UK. So if attractions such as Drayton Manor are to survive in an increasingly-competitive environment, then innovative thinking and strategic forward-planning has to be an essential part of our corporate make-up. But it is a fact of life that, economically, you can't always have what you want when you want it – hence, my vision having been on ice for some time.

In creating one of the country's most-visited inland theme parks, we have invested well over £40 million and since the 80s we have injected at least £2 million every year on introducing new rides and other attractions. That has been money well spent, but just as parents who visit our park can't always afford to buy their children all the latest designer gear, then we, also, have had to put some projects on the back-burner and wait for another day.

However, I believe the time is now approaching when we will implement the next phase of our redevelopment programme - an ambitious project in which we will commit a further large sum of money over a 9-to-10 year plan, one which will eventually transform Drayton Manor from a "day out" theme park to that of a holiday destination.

Already, we have received planning permission from Lichfield District Council to construct, on existing parkland within Drayton Manor, an 86-bedroom hotel, complete with spa, gymnasium, function suite, restaurant and an imaginative sky-bar, which would overlook the grounds. But our "dream" is to create a spectacular new water park, complete with 40+ self-catering log cabin chalets that would be available all-the-year-round. Added to these facilities will be up to 150 Log Effect mobile bungalow/cabins which will be useful to families staying over weekends & summer holidays, which will, I am sure, complement the hotel, making Drayton Manor a true destination resort comparable with many other theme parks worldwide.

It is hoped that construction of the hotel could commence as early as 2007/8. It will have three-star status – but will feature four-star touches. The water park will come later – but already we have exhibited our proposals in order to give members of the public an opportunity to air their views, and Lichfield District

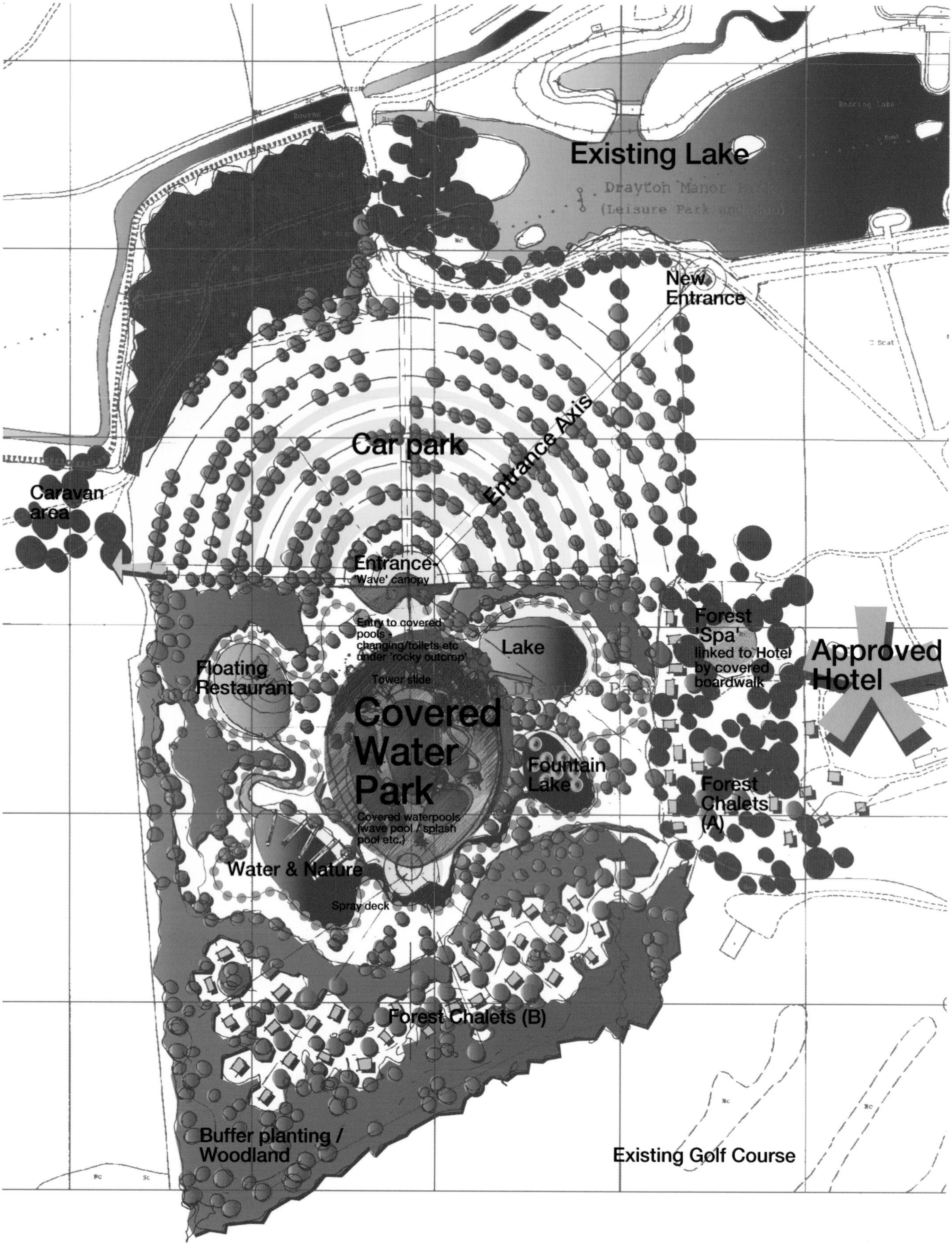

Existing Lake
Drayton Manor Park
(Leisure Park and Zoo)
New Entrance
Car park
Entrance Axis
Caravan area
Entrance-
'Wave' canopy
Entry to covered pools - changing/toilets etc under 'rocky outcrop'
Tower slide
Lake
Floating Restaurant
Forest 'Spa' linked to Hotel by covered boardwalk
Approved Hotel
Covered Water Park
Covered waterpools (wave pool / splash pool etc.)
Fountain Lake
Forest Chalets (A)
Water & Nature
Spray deck
Forest Chalets (B)
Buffer planting / Woodland
Existing Golf Course

Concept Masterplan > **Land at Drayton Manor**

Drayton Manor Park

| Team MC/CJH | Feb 2005 | 1:12500 @A1 | Pegasus Urban Design | drwg. BIR.1340_01

Council has agreed to support the expansion as part of its "preferred options" for future local development.

Our plan is to provide a water park and forest chalets on 32-acres to the west of the existing theme park, making full use of mature woodland to create an environmentally-friendly development, which would be sympathetic to its surroundings. The water park, which will include a large domed swimming pool and various water slides, will be available to the hotel and log cabin patrons all year round and will be accessed by a covered walkway It will also feature a mezzanine with gym equipment and a cafe – but the area will not include any additional theme park rides.

Such a scheme will also enable us to expand our facilities for camping and touring caravans.

So when's it all going to happen? There's a long way to go yet. But I would imagine that when Drayton Manor celebrates its Diamond Anniversary in 2010 the theme park will be looking a lot different than it does today! For my own part, I have witnessed many significant changes since coming on board 40 years ago as a 16-year-old. That's "coming on board" as a member of the staff – for don't forget I first moved to Drayton Manor as a young baby when my parents acquired the property in 1949.

I can remember right from the age of ten wanting to be a part of Drayton Manor – though my father says I was helping him with its construction well before then. However, I must admit I don't recall too much about transporting bricks and rubble about in a children's wheelbarrow. But, then, I was only three years old!

Mind you, I have always been very practical and mechanically-minded – inheriting, I like to think, the skills of my father and both my grandfathers. By the age of nine I could drive my mother's Ford 100E car and when I was 14 Dad bought me an Austin 7 (1933 saloon). Today, motoring is still a passion of mine and I have eight vehicles, including a sprint car built from the body of that Austin 7, but using many other bits and pieces from other cars as well. Building cars set me up with the welding and metalwork skills that in my early days helped establish myself in the business!

When it came to leave school, however, I had a choice of going into the Army, where I could have developed my knowledge of electrical engineering, or going to catering college – in essence, following in my father's footsteps. I finally decided on catering college because, although I knew I would be happy enough to be involved on the practical side of the business, I considered that ultimately I would like to drive forward the catering business, building on what was then a small part of the firm and developing it into a renowned catering company.

In 1965 I started a two-year course at Birmingham College of Food, during which time I was cook, chef and bottle-washer! It was a thoroughly enjoyable experience and I have a high regard for the way in which the college operates. The qualifications I gained there were invaluable when the time came for me to become a member of the Hotel Catering International Management Association.

When I wasn't at college, I was learning "the trade" at week-ends, working at the park. I can remember a member of the catering staff, Mrs Edden, teaching me the art of frying chips. I remember she always liked a cigarette – but that's something health & safety rules would never allow today. If I wasn't in the kitchens, then I would be helping my mother serve afternoon teas – all 2,000 of them to children who were, perhaps, on their only day out that year!

I left college in 1967 and started work at Drayton Manor as an assistant catering manager, first of all, under my uncle, Norman Cartlidge, and then George Caddy. He was every inch the professional caterer and together we often worked an 80-90 hour week. Not only performing catering duties but planning and restructuring the layout of the kitchens themselves, updating the equipment that had been the backbone of the company since my father had purchased it many years before. One item, a hot cupboard (built in 1935 for the Daimler Car Factory in Coventry), is now too old to be used, but parts of it still exist.

As time moved on, catering developed into banqueting and Drayton Manor became a second "home" to thousands of workers from Greater Birmingham as its welcoming environment proved an ideal location for their annual dinners and dances. It is not unusual to hold 500 banqueting functions a year, Christmas past and Christmas present being particularly hectic times. Often we will serve seven tons of turkey over the festive period!

The popularity of such events, however, relies heavily upon the level of customer service that guests receive and I am delighted that our catering staff, many of whom are following in the footsteps of their own parents and even grandparents by working at Drayton Manor, are frequently complimented for their high standards of efficiency. Current catering manager John Price has a team to be proud off.

Drayton really is a family business – not just from the Bryan's point of view but also from that of many staff members. For example, I have worked at the park for 40 years – and all that time there has been a member of the Deeming family here as well. Sam Deeming was head chef for many years, now his daughter-in-law, Linda, occupies the same role. She has had her daughter employed both as a waitress and as a member of the catering staff – three generations in the same department. That really is something special!

There's no denying that when the banqueting season is in full flow, behind-the-scenes activity can be rather frenetic – just like you see in all those television cookery programmes! But one of the most unflappable people I have ever met was the late Jim Towers, a former Lieutenant Colonel in the Army Catering Corps. Jim was catering manager here for about 18 years. He was an eloquent man who ran his department with typical military efficiency and it was a pleasure for me to learn and benefit from his considerable experience and knowledge.

All this time, however, I was also more than happy to help out on the practical side of the business as well. Sometimes I would drive the snake train, mow the grass, help out at the Chairlift and carry out whatever repair work was necessary. Even today, I love engineering, whether it is getting involved with the creation and installation of our latest Big Rides, re-building one of my cars or simply just a DIY exercise.

I also sometimes carried out duties as an animal handler at the park's zoo – and I have the scars to prove it from close up encounters with razor-sharp bear claws and the like. It wasn't all pain, though, I found love there as well! I was 23 at the time and started to date one of the keepers, Lynne, who has been my wife since 1971. It wasn't exactly love at first sight, however. I was wearing a hand-made yellow-and-red pom-pom hat at the time (well, it was winter!) and Lynne thought I looked a "right walley."

Meeting at a leisure park, however, is something of a theme that runs through our family.

Mother and father came together through California-in-England; my son George met his wife, Eve, while she was working on the catering staff at Drayton – and they spent their honeymoon at Disney World! – and my elder son William also first met his wife, Claire, while she was on the staff as well and they, too, enjoyed their honeymoon in Florida at Disney World and The Keys. Talk about taking a "busman's holiday." All good for the business, though!

However, when the time finally came for me to decide which road to take, I opted for the catering/banqueting arm of the business. Today's youngsters take their burgers and fizzy drinks for granted but I can remember the time when tea was served from large urns and there wasn't such a thing as fast food or microwaves. In fact, it wasn't until about 1979-80 that we introduced microwaves to our restaurants. Then we installed a bank of microwaves, each one cooking six pre-boxed burgers at a time. Today, we serve over 1,000 burgers an hour. The "fries" (as opposed to chips) came later – after we discovered, during a trip to Belgium, just how popular they were. McDonalds brought them in as well, but from the USA.

Old-fashioned fish and chips, however, have always been a favourite with visitors to the park and even though we offer a wide range of food in our various eating outlets, they still remain as popular as ever. However, with today's emphasis being on healthy eating, visitors can rest assured that there are plenty of options for them to choose from, including traditional cooked food, wraps and fresh salads. In fact, the choice is huge – right from cafeterias that serve English breakfasts all day long to a Pizza restaurant set in a rainforest environment!

Just what will be on the menu when our new hotel opens, though, we will have to wait and see.